# BEYOND
## THE
# SCIENCE KIT

# BEYOND
## THE
# SCIENCE KIT

Edited by
**Wendy Saul** *and* **Jeanne Reardon**

**HEINEMANN**
Portsmouth, NH

Heinemann
A division of Reed Elsevier Inc.
361 Hanover Street
Portsmouth, NH 03801-3912
*Offices and agents throughout the world*

"Writing Eco-Mysteries", © 1996 by Twig C. George.

The material in this volume is based upon work supported by the National Science Foundation under grant number TPE-9353454. Any opinions, findings, and conclusions or recommendations expressed in this material are those of the authors and do not necessarily reflect the views of the National Science Foundation.

**Cataloging-in-Publication Data is on file at the Library of Congress.**

Editor: Toby Gordon
Production: J.B. Tranchemontagne
Manufacturing: Louise Richardson
Cover Design: Darci Mehall
Cover Photo: Barbara Bourne

Printed in the United States of America on acid-free paper
04  03          **EB**        7  8

For Elyse Eidman-Aadahl
Friend, Colleague, Mentor

# Contents

*Section I: Inquiry into Inquiry*     1

1    **Teacher Bones: An Introduction**     3
*Wendy Saul*

2    **It Takes More than a Kit**     12
*Jeanne Reardon*

*Section II: What's Important?*     31

3    **The Building Blocks of Science**     33
*Carole Roberts*

4    **"There's a Squid in Mrs. Bunn's Classroom!"**     44
*Debra Bunn*

5    **The Reason for Reasoning**     54
*Linda Davis*

6    **Connections**     68
*Barbara Caplan*

7    **Working in Community**     79
*Stephanie Terry*

*Section III: Making It Work*                                    91

8    How I *Really* Plan                                         93
     *Donna Dieckman*

9    A Year in the Life of a First-Grade Class                  101
     *Carol Flicker*

10   Consumer Testing:  Children Working on                     119
     Authentic Science Problems
     *Jeanne Reardon*

11   Looking for Hope in All the Wrong Places                   135
     *Mary Beth Johnson*

12   Writing Eco-Mysteries                                      144
     *Twig C. George*

13   The Kids' Inquiry Conference:                              167
     Not Just Another Science Fair
     *Barbara Bourne*

     About the Contributors                                     189

# Inquiry into Inquiry

# 1 Wendy Saul

# Teacher Bones: An Introduction

Years ago, as a teacher in New York City, I remember my supervisor coming in for both planned and unannounced observations. I hated those observations, not because I hated her or my ratings, but because of our post-observation conferences; the discussion was always far from what I saw as important in my classroom. She attended wholly to the lesson—the clarity and appropriateness of my objectives, the pacing, how questions enhanced student outcomes—whereas my focus was on the values that shaped my performance. I wanted to think about and be evaluated on how these values were realized.

My supervisor had her forms to fill out, but being "open," she tried to include a question or two addressed to my preoccupation with "big ideas": Were students becoming more independent learners? Were they understanding literature as a human construction? Her concession was of little use. Values, I soon realized, are not always evident in a single lesson. Furthermore, learning something about the progress I had made in promoting my vision of classroom life was surely nothing a supervisor could see at a glance. Was Ramon more engaged than he had been a month ago? Did the work we undertook on point of view have an effect on student writing? These were questions that needed to be answered over time.

The essays in *Beyond the Science Kit* are about values. In this case these values are being used to drive science instruction in remarkable ways, and so the book appears to be, and finally is, a book about more, and better, science teaching. To achieve this clear and practical science orientation I have eliminated sections of the teachers' original manuscripts. All of the authors of these essays, for example, wrote about how they were affected by their participation in the Elementary Science Integration Project (ESIP), a National Science Foundation-funded program designed to enhance science learning across the K–8 curriculum. Whenever possible I edited out these sections. Both as a writer and a teacher educator I did not want to produce a book with cult-like qualities—join us and we'll take you there.

But as I look at these extracted sections literally scattered across my desk, I hear an old question resurfacing. Have I inadvertently eliminated what really matters? In retrospect, I believe that the authors of these essays wanted to write about ESIP because it is a shorthand way of describing what they have come to believe and value. And these beliefs and values explain, in large measure, what and why and how they teach.

## Time

In the demanding, beehive-like atmosphere of the school, it is hard to find time. Even experienced teachers juggle and push their way through the curriculum, trying to eke out thirty minutes here and there for a class walk or a poem about a long-awaited snow. After-school hours not spent preparing for the children are regularly occupied with in-service activities planned to meet institutional goals and objectives. There is little or no time for reflection built into the job, and little sense that a teacher might value time for conversation and thought about "big," not obviously utilitarian, ideas.

Hungry for this kind of thinking time, I left the classroom and found a job at a university. I now work longer hours, but I find time in the day to think, and write and plan my classes. ESIP was, from the beginning, an attempt to give K–8 teachers the kind of time I enjoy as a faculty member. It also represented a commitment on the part of participating teachers to think and write about their practice.

In 1990, twenty-six teachers, half of whom had a strong background in science and half in some other area of the curriculum, generally language arts, joined the Elementary Science Integration Project. The idea was not to teach content per se, but rather to present participants with a rich array of intellectually challenging and vibrant speakers—scientists, science writers, developmental psychologists, teacher researchers—and to better understand what sense these teachers made of the experience, both during the summer and throughout the school year. How did the ideas encountered connect to one another? How did they connect to experiences in the K–8 classroom? What contradictions seemed evident? What ideas seemed particularly appealing?

Each afternoon participants engaged in informal investigations of particular science phenomena, developing meaningful, testable questions and answering them. They also spent time examining and commenting on children's science-related trade books. Teachers kept detailed journals of their reactions (see Baker and Saul 1994) and gathered material from their students for their presentations and publications.

It was a summer of surprises. I had thought that I was there to learn something about how talented, experienced practitioners made sense of the ideas the educational enterprise thrust upon them. What happened, however, was far more interesting and compelling. "Now I remember why I went into teaching twenty years ago," said one veteran teacher. "It's so liberating to be with other people who love teaching," another noted. Several were moved to tears as they wrote about the affirmation they felt within the group.

## Values

It is difficult to enter into a community where expectations are high and there is no formula, no clear-cut path to achievement. Working without guidelines is at once frustrating and challenging. This tension is both the problem with and the gift of ESIP. Teachers, anxious not to disappoint, look around for models. Whom do I admire here? What have they done? How did they get there? Finally, each finds a way back to him- or herself.

In order to grow we have to begin where we are with the knowledge, experiences, and feelings that seem most solid. When I am down to my teacher bare bones, who am I? To support and nourish growth, teacher educators also have to start with these bare bones, with the teacher's sense of what is most important. For teachers like those in this book, a great deal of time has been spent looking outside, accommodating, building on other people's visions, attending to the expressed needs of children, parents, and administrators. ESIP provided (and still provides) a place where they could attend to themselves as professionals. In other words, ESIP serves in this essay, and in those that follow, as a shorthand call for a particular kind of opportunity. Teachers need time to think about science in a setting that is not task oriented. They need time to consider questions such as, How does science work for scientists? For children? For themselves?

Often teachers begin by viewing science as objective, as the province of people concerned more with facts and less with communication. I worry that many of the programs now available reinforce this image. Instead we need experiences that invite teachers to see that, fundamentally, science springs from human curiosity, a curiosity familiar to every thinking practitioner. When one is able to see him- or herself as a producer rather than a consumer of science, the entire picture changes. For the educator who recognizes, owns, and values that curiosity, the other pieces fall easily into place:

- Science is seen as interesting.
- If I can think, I can do it.
- My students, if allowed to pursue their own curiosities, will also be interested in science.
- My students and I have been missing something really good, and I'd best make up for lost time.

I have written about ESIP in some detail because the model is not a difficult one for any university or school system to adopt. Moreover, if a teacher is disciplined and lucky, she might be able to create a situation in which she finds the support, time, and space needed for reflection. The point here is that such opportunities are the right of every teacher. It makes our work possible.

## Science as Inquiry

A main goal of schools, and the overarching purpose of science in the elementary grades, is to teach students to think. Science thinking is a particular kind of thinking; it involves asking and attempting to answer questions about the physical world, questions about which there is evidence. Some call this process of asking and answering questions *inquiry*.

Inquiry may be becoming one of those words that through overuse is in danger of losing its meaning. However, like whole language or critical thinking, it deserves better. Rather than generating a definition, it is probably more useful to begin with an experience. Years ago in a teacher workshop I was given a tub of water, a roll of aluminum foil, and a partner. We were told to make a foil boat and to see how much weight we could get it to hold. What I remember most about the experience was the sense of total involvement. For all intents and purposes my partner and I might have been alone in the room. I had no sense of time passing, no interest in anything but that boat, the water, and the weights.

We began by experimenting with the shape of our boat, and decided finally on a raft. We messed with the placement of objects on the boat and with the shape of the weights we used. I remember scrambling through my pocketbook to find my heavy set of keys—I wanted flat, heavy objects to see if they would balance differently than the weights the instructor had given us. When the instructor said it was time to clean up, I was annoyed. I hadn't finished. I had more questions.

This experience occurred over twenty years ago, yet I can recall with absolute clarity the room, the water, the aluminum foil, and the balances that we used to measure our "load." I can also remember thinking for days afterwards about why the boats worked as they did. And later, reading a book on displacement, I was able to substitute mentally the illustrations on the page with my own image of what it meant to see the various boats I constructed that day sink. Inquiry, when it works, is powerful stuff.

Inquiry is realized in the coming together of material and learner. An interesting material, such as bubbles or water, can draw an otherwise reluctant child in, and do much to promote good questions. Conversely, curious, probing children regularly find much to examine in the most ordinary of circumstances and substances. Good teachers recognize the ways materials and curiosity relate, and help students as they tentatively or bullishly try to connect their own questions to ways of "finding out." They also work with children to "make sense" of what they find and construct arguments that seem convincing to others in their scientific community.

There are two important points. The first is that the engagement that characterizes inquiry is very much in the mind of the scientist, child, or adult. The second point is that if teachers have no sense of what inquiry feels like, they have neither reason nor the means for promoting it. The teachers represented in this volume recognize and have built their science classrooms with inquiry as a standard. They encourage connections between students' questions and the mandated curriculum, and would now find it impossible to simply plod or gallop along lesson by lesson, ignoring children's responses and queries. In this sense they have moved beyond the science kit or textbook.

## Marketing Inquiry

Inquiry is an attitude, an approach to learning acted out through the use of materials. Every time I hear a textbook or kit publisher claim that theirs is an inquiry-based program, I am puzzled. Inquiry exists finally in the heads of the teachers and children who construct meaning out of the materials that textbook and kit manufacturers have supplied. At best, these manufacturers have made good guesses about what materials will engage the children for whom the kits were purchased. But when the exploration of materials is tightly tied to a particular learning sequence or set of lesson plans, these kits take us further from, not closer to, authentic science.

Inquiry, that knowledge of and interest in authentic curiosities and methods, is key to the kind of science we advocate in the essays that follow. But inquiry is not enough. There are scientists and science educators, for instance, who understand inquiry inside and out, but when it comes to working with children or designing curriculum, they fail. There are at least three reasons for that failure: 1) kid connections are not invited nor built upon; 2) programs reflect little trust in students or their teachers; and 3) revision is not considered key to scientific reasoning. Inquiry, in order to survive, must be nourished by relevance, trust, and revision.

Publishers, in order to make a kit or textbook economically viable, must reach a large audience. Most of the large ones have sought to design materials that will sell well in Arizona, New York, Texas, and Illinois. Also, in an attempt to reach the widest audience they have focused on topics or units that can be taught at any time of the year. The problem, of course, is that such programs ignore the material resources as well as the questions and background knowledge children living with those materials have in place. The fourth graders, the children of Chesapeake Bay watermen, who live with tides and oyster shells and sandy soil, bring very different experiences to science than do children living on the Hopi Reservation, where water is scarce.

Looking at the lists of questions designed to promote inquiry in kits and textbooks, I am struck by the ways in which certain lists seem inviting and others are clearly less so. Surely this has to do with numerous factors: personal memory, aversions to particular smells or tastes, access to background information. Susan Blunck and Robert Yager have made this point in print and action through their Chautauqua Program (1990). Science, they tell us, needs to be local, personal, and relevant. If a kit or a textbook does not invite children and teachers to connect what they know and have available to them, their science studies will be less robust and meaningful than they could and should be. Conversely, if teachers can help students make such connections and move beyond generic lessons, the science they teach will come alive for the children in their charge.

Trust is another factor that is absolutely necessary if teachers and children are to move beyond kit-based instruction. I have worked with smart, scientifically skilled people designing curriculum for children. Invariably they begin with their own excitement about a given problem, ask fascinating questions about the concept or material in question, and then create a series of activities that help answer their questions. The problem, of course, is that they are working with *their* questions. They don't trust children to have questions of their own, and they don't trust themselves to build on student questions in a creative way. Moreover, they are scared silly about the possibility that children will come up with an "answer" or theory that is scientifically incorrect.

The results of programs born from a lack of trust are widespread and familiar: narrow goals and objectives, lock-step lesson plans, and limited materials. Scientists know, without a doubt, that people working through real science problems need time for their own confusion. Moreover, they tend to regard their own mistakes with respect and sometimes fondness—they know that they learn from investigation and exploration. But in constructing a program for youngsters, those values are often subsumed by other values, such as efficiency and correctness. Even relatively inexpensive items that are part of a kit—straws, tape, beans, baking soda—are often meted out so that no child can practice his investigation more than once. A child who uses materials "incorrectly" or inefficiently is often downgraded for deviating from the prescribed directions, or kept from participating in further investigations. Even teachers, in both written guidebooks and training workshops, are discouraged from attending to their own and their students' queries.

A "trusting" kit program would provide enough of what is needed to invite the happy exploration of alternatives. Such a program would also allow a teacher actively using the kit to keep it for as long as it is needed in order to adapt it and connect it to the world. In the best of circumstances such an educator would be credited, not chastised, for the involvement with science she has promoted.

The third element missing from most textbook or kit programs has to do with the way the scientific process is being conceptualized and popularized. I call this the "hypothesis syndrome." Students have somehow come to believe that the job of a scientist is to ask a question, correctly guess the answer, and then "do something" to convince others that their guess was correct. Although this scenario may mimic the reporting structure adopted in scientific journals, it does not, in fact, mimic scientific research.

Science begins with curiosity and investigation. The questions a fledgling or educated scientist asks depend, in large measure, on the background knowledge that the scientist has. In this sense, experimentation is essentially a form of revision. Anna, a third grader who likes plants, looks at a pussy willow and remembers that it is one of the earliest plants to bloom in her yard. She comes up with a "hypothesis" that large budded plants bloom earlier than small budded plants. She takes notes on which plants bloom when. The forsythia blooms early, as does the magnolia. Now, as a victim of the hypothesis syndrome, Anna might become discouraged with the data she has collected—the forsythia has small buds and blooms early. That means that her hypothesis is wrong and her experiment "failed."

But in a classroom where revision rather than correct hypotheses are valued, Anna now finds herself in a position to ask a new and better question. Inquiry isn't a student's ability to guess correctly. Rather, it is the urge that sends us back to rethink our experiments and investigations, to revise our thoughts and answers. Without an appreciation of revision, inquiry does not, and cannot, exist.

This takes us back to kits and textbooks. How often does a kit program offer students the means and teachers the encouragement to revisit activities in the classroom? By pushing teacher and student through a set of activities, we have robbed them of the opportunity to do that which is most essential to science—learn from mistakes, control an experiment more rigorously, observe and record more carefully.

The goal of this book is not to encourage teachers to dispense with kits, but rather to encourage them and their students to see kits as a beginning, not an end. Essentially, the question these essays try to answer is how have teachers, some more, some less familiar with science knowledge, turned around their science teaching to make themselves and the children in their charge producers as well as consumers of science knowledge. As teachers inquire into their own teaching, they become more able to help children with the practice of inquiry. And finally, it is an appreciation and delight in inquiry that leads back again and again to science.

The essays in this book are divided into three sections. The first section, this essay and Jeanne Reardon's piece on science kits, sets out the problem that the rest of the book addresses. Mine is from a university and project director's perspective; Jeanne's is a concrete and powerful explanation of the problem and the solution from inside a classroom.

The second section of the book has to do with what I referred to earlier as the "bare bones" of teaching. These essays, both individually and in the aggregate, offer a glimpse of what five remarkable teachers see as the place they began, the solid matter upon which they were able to build a dynamic and thoughtful science program. These essays are designed to help talk about the values upon which inquiry-based science has been built.

The third section offers readers a day-to-day sense of what it looks like when teachers successfully help students forge connections between science and their daily lives. These are teachers who trust their students and who make time in the classroom for revision. In that sense, these are teachers who have moved beyond hands-on, beyond the textbook, beyond the science kit.

Although there are many "how-tos" embedded in the essays, we ask that you not read this book as a how-to guide. The exciting part about the science we advocate has to do with the ways you will make it your own. Make time to think and remember and connect. Without time to rethink, to construct and reconstruct ideas, without time to connect your own head and heart, neither science nor head nor heart matter. In science, as in all things, time for reflection and research is the method, the means, the enabler. Giving yourself and your students time is the "big value" about which we write.

## Bibliography

Baker, L. and W. Saul. 1994. "Considering Science and Language Arts Connections: A Study of Teacher Cognition." *Journal of Research in Science Teaching* 31(9): 1023–1037.

Blunck, S.M. and R.E. Yager. 1990. "The Iowa Chautauqua Program: A Model for Improving Science in the Elementary School." *Journal of Elementary Science Education* 2(2): 3–9.

Saul, W. et al. 1993. *Science Workshop*. Portsmouth, NH: Heinemann.

# 2 Jeanne Reardon

# It Takes More than a Kit

*Tomorrow when I go outside I'm going to put two thermometers in my mitten—one with the glass next to my mitten and one with the glass next to me.*

Kevin, grade 1

Kevin is a scientist, not because he has a thermometer or because he can read a thermometer, but because he is pursuing his question systematically. Kevin's question is part of a larger question, "How come mittens are warm?" Right now Kevin wants to know, "Is the thermometer measuring the temperature of my hand or the temperature of the mitten?" Other children are wondering, if mittens really are warm, *when* are mittens warm? How can you keep the cold air out of mittens? If I put a rubber band around the opening will my mitten stay warm inside?

Our class and other first-grade classes in my school district are studying weather. The school system has sent out weather kits to our classrooms, giving us plenty of thermometers. We also have the teacher's guide that accompanies the kit. If you are familiar with *Weather and Me: Field Test Edition*, or the commercial edition, *Weather* (NSRC), then you must be thinking, "That's not in the guide. Where did she get those questions?" You would be right and wrong. This is not the science *found* in the weather kit or guide, but it is science that *came from* the kit. Let me explain.

The materials in the kit and the guide provide a catalyst to start me thinking about weather science. As I read the guide I reflect on science, children, and learning. I have a conversation with the guide, and from this conversation our science grows. Just as children think better when their hands are in science, I and other teachers often find it easier to plan when there is a published plan and materials in our hands to react to. In this sense our science comes from the kit. On the other hand, if I insisted that the students do precisely what the kit prescribes them to do, the students would need to put away their questions and curiosities. If we followed this guide as it is written the children would have few opportunities to practice science. Our science is not found in the kit or the accompanying guide.

In this chapter I share my thoughts as I plan for the weather unit. Science kits have become the children's science program in my school district and in many schools across the country. Since we use the kits, my thoughts focus on them and how they affect children, teachers, and science learning. Science kits are not a new idea. In the days after Sputnik, kits were seen as the solution to schools' failure to teach science. Now there is a new push "to be first in the world in science and mathematics by the year 2000," and science kits are back. My hope is that this time kits will provide some of the support teachers need to help children learn science and confront the world as scientists. My concern is that the kits produce harmful side effects.

## What Kinds of Support Do Teachers Need?

What kinds of support do teachers need? Clearly we need materials, and kits answer this need. The weather kit in our room right now contains materials to use with the lessons in the guide—a good start on the materials we will use as we explore weather. This is the third of four kits that the school system will rotate through my first-grade classroom this year. At the end of eight weeks I will send it back to be refilled before it goes on to another classroom. Having the kit materials on hand saves me time and money.

Teachers desperately need time to meet and talk with other teachers and scientists. We need to engage in science ourselves and reflect on what it is we do as scientists. To be effective reading and writing teachers we need to read and write. We do not need to write and publish novels, essays, poems, journals, or biographies. But we must write to become aware of how we write, to know ourselves as writers, to be a part of the community of writers. We do not need to practice laboratory science, but we need to think and analyze and solve problems scientifically. We need to recognize science problems when we meet them. Kits are unable to provide for this need.

Finally, teachers need annotated bibliographies of tradebooks, descriptions of research, professional journals, books, and time to read and investigate. Some kits provide bibliographies. A guide may be useful too, especially when traveling in an unknown land. Teaching science is an unknown land for many of us. Even teachers with extensive science backgrounds find themselves traveling out of their familiar areas of science expertise. We look to guides for support.

## Having a Conversation with the Guide

### Reflections on Children, Science, and Learning

I wrote that as I read a guide I think about science, children, and learning. Everything I do in our classroom springs from my beliefs about children. Before I describe my conversation with a guide you need to know how I think about children. I find children to be capable and thoughtful. I have great confidence in children as meaning makers. I know that children come to school with a body of science-related information. They know that weather changes from day to day, from season to season. They know that the weather affects the clothing they wear and the activities they pursue. It would be a waste of time to teach what they already know. The children bring with them the curiosity and adventuresome spirit of science, but they do not yet have the critical edge of adult scientists. They are not as practiced in turning observations into wonderings, in seeing patterns, or in making connections among their observations.

I believe that when children are given many opportunities to investigate their own questions they not only build concepts, but they will revise their concepts. I am not afraid to let them speak or write down "wrong science." I believe that science talk and science writing is crucial to the development of scientific understanding. I have found that children extend their understanding, and make connections and applications when they engage in long-term investigations. I do not believe that science is ever completed. It is never "finished" or "done." There is always more. That is part of the fun (and part of the frustration) of learning. I am very uncomfortable with neat little lessons where children follow the directions to someone else's science—and believe they are finished when the final step is completed.

My assumptions about children and science have led me to define some of the elements I consider essential to a good science program (see Reardon 1993). I believe that children must have time to explore and investigate problems and materials of their choosing. They also need response, challenge, and support from their scientific community. This means they talk about what they are doing in science, how they are working, what they notice, what surprises them, what problems and questions they have, and the steps they will take next. They increase their knowledge of science and their repertoire of problem-solving techniques as they read, listen, observe, and are questioned by other scientists at work.

This probably has a familiar sound to many teachers as we think of what it is we do to develop a community of readers and writers. We give children time to explore, investigate, and select from a variety of written texts. Children receive responses, challenge, and support from their reading and writing community. Children and adults talk about what they are reading and writing, how they read, what they notice; they explain the meanings they take from the book, discuss their questions, surprises . . .

## An Overview of the Teacher's Guide

I have read twenty to twenty-five guides that accompany science kits. I even talk to myself as I read these guides. I pick up the guide as I would pick up a catalogue; I hold the guide and let the pages slip away from under my left thumb. I glance at the pages as they slip by, stopping when something catches my interest. I see blackline masters to copy, a bibliography, and pages and pages of lessons with numbers marching down the left side, showing the steps in preparation and procedures to be followed. There are photographs, drawings, and stories. I reach the front of the guide and find the table of contents. Now I am ready for some serious reading.

As I read a guide I note its philosophy, content, format, and usability. Many guides state the program's philosophy in the introduction. All of the philosophies I have read speak to hands-on investigations by children. They emphasize process, scientific attitude, and concept development rather than content knowledge. As I read, I look to see if the philosophy expressed in the introduction is reflected in the activities set out for the children. I look for child identification of problems and child-generated investigations, and child-selected materials, tests, and record keeping formats.

The guides I have read contain many pages of activity lessons for the teacher to follow. Some have little more. Other guides include thumbnail biographies, poetry, annotated bibliographies of tradebooks, extensive assessment forms, letters to parents, addresses of additional resources and background information for teachers. Those guides with a variety of content can become resources to teachers rather than scripts for teaching lessons.

I read through the whole weather guide and ask myself, "What does the guide think is important for children to know about weather?" I read the introduction and goals. "Oh," I say. "They already know that. What else does this guide set out to do?" Collect and organize data. "That's important." I read on and ask, "Which of these are really skills?" "When does a scientist use a thermometer? What is the reason?" I look through the lessons to see how the children will be using the tools of science. I think about how the lessons relate to each other. I skim the lessons and ask, "Are the children always following directions?" "How much time do children have for their *own* explorations, their *own* questions?" "Which of these activities are important, and which should be omitted?"

Teacher's guides exert a powerful influence on the teaching of science in elementary schools. The guide often defines science for both student and teacher. My school district brought teachers from a cluster of four elementary schools together partway through the weather unit. We shared ideas and talked about what we were doing. Most of these teachers were enthusiastic about the weather kit. They were looking for support in teaching science and they followed the guide closely. All of these teachers are women who enjoy teaching. They are hard working and committed to teaching the weather unit well. A conversation with them includes questions and comments like these:

"What lesson are you on?"

"How many lessons do you do a week?"

"The kids like the weather stamps. I leave them out so they can use
        them."

"Have you done Lesson 8, Predicting Temperatures? My principal wanted
        to observe me teaching science and I did the lesson for my
        evaluation observation."

"How do you keep the kids from changing their predictions after they fill
        in the worksheet? They want to get it right."

"The kids really liked pouring the water through the cloth, but I don't
        know if their measurements were accurate."

"Could your kids pull the shoestrings through their thermometers to set
        them?"

"We made cotton clouds in art and copied a poem to go with them."

The comments and questions I hear focus on the lessons, what the children like, how the teachers and students are proceeding through the lessons, and on arts and crafts or language extensions. I rarely hear the children's questions and connections, the meaning children are making from the lessons, the children's plans, or comments about their science explorations. These teachers measure their success as science teachers by how well they and the children follow the guide. This is interesting because these same teachers do not define themselves as successful mathematics or reading teachers by their use of a mathematics or reading guide. They count themselves as successful reading teachers because their students enjoy reading, understand what they read, talk about books, and know themselves as readers. They consider themselves successful mathematics teachers when their students enjoy playing with the ideas of mathematics, recognize mathematics as useful, and use mathematics to solve their problems. What is it about the science kit guide that gives it such authority? Why is it so influential? I go back to the guide to search for answers.

## Attending to Procedure

When I look at guides I am always struck by the large amount of space given to the *procedures* to be followed. (These are procedures for "somebody else's" science.) When we were students and took laboratory science courses we carefully followed procedures. If we followed the procedures closely then we would get the correct result. That was what science was about—getting the correct result. For many teachers hands-on science *is* procedures. It is the procedure section of lessons that dominates books of science experiments and most of the guides found in science kits. Perhaps it is the dominance of procedures that gives science kit guides such authority and power.

If we think more about the function of procedure in science, then guides may lose some of their power. Replication is crucial in science. Being able to describe in accurate detail the steps taken in an investigation means another person can replicate one's work. Often scientists share a discovery by describing their procedure. The procedure describes the scientist's work. I believe that the important part of replication for children comes in telling and writing, "This is what I did . . . and this is what I noticed. . . ." When children are looking so closely at "what" they did that they are able to describe their procedure, they begin to think about what has happened in a new way. This is when children make connections and build concepts. It is not procedure per se that is important. It is being able to describe one's own procedure that is important. Science is not found in procedures; it is found in questions. That is how I think and talk to myself. It is a replay of one of many conversations I had in response to a guide. I do not want a guide to be in charge of the children's science. I want the children to have that power.

## Looking Closely at the Lessons

After I have studied the guide as a whole I look closely at separate lessons. Some of the teacher's manuals have very structured lessons. Others, like *Windows on Science*™, give the teacher more flexibility in guiding the children's investigations. There are three science questions I ask when I read a lesson. As a teacher, my questions focus on real problem solving, relevancy, and rigor. My first question is, "Does this lesson engage children in *real* problem solving?" Is there a problem, or just a procedure to follow? Is it an authentic problem? Is it a science problem? Next, I ask, "Is the lesson *relevant* to the children, to their experience and environment?" Lastly, I ask, "Is the lesson scientifically *rigorous*?" Are the children doing what practicing scientists do—asking questions, talking, writing, challenging each other, explaining, testing, comparing, thinking, confirming, revising, planning?

Those were my thoughts as I began reading lessons from the weather kit guide. I turned to the thermometer lessons. "Thermometers are real science tools. There are so many possibilities," I thought. "Ohhh, no . . . the kids will just be making paper thermometers to set and read." I read down the list of materials and preparations and came to the procedure list. "What a script, it even tells me to be sure the kids put their names on the back of the paper thermometer. Not much going on here," I mutter. "I wonder when the kids will get to the real thermometers?" I thought about my criteria: real, relevant, and rigorous. There can't be authentic problems to solve when all you have in front of you is a nonfunctioning, paper thermometer. This lesson has nothing to do with the lives of children—it won't be relevant to them.

This paper thermometer activity reminds me of children practicing letters and sounds out of context so that eventually they will be ready for a real book. But this is, in fact, worse. At least children have a chance to listen to real books, look at them, and check them out from the library. In this case, the children do not hold a real thermometer until after they have sufficient practice with the paper ones. They are given two more "activity sheets" that have printed thermometers to read. The children fill in the blank for the temperature and write if they think that temperature is hot or cold. All of this is done without hands-on experience measuring hot and cold with real thermometers. Accurate and *meaningful* reading of a thermometer is an important science skill, but should we have children practice reading a printed paper thermometer? We have learned in the teaching of reading that skills taught in isolation are frequently unavailable to children when they need to use them in authentic reading situations.

My thoughts move to the scientist's use of thermometers. The guide is careful to have the teacher explain to the students that these are "model" thermometers; that real thermometers have fluid inside that moves up or down depending on the temperature. The shoelace on the model thermometers represents the fluid that is in a real thermometer. The use of models in science is an interesting topic worth thinking about. When do scientists use models? Why? What kind of models do scientists use? It is hard to imagine a scientist making a model like this paper thermometer to understand how a thermometer works. Authenticity is a concept I keep returning to as I read guides.

I read other thermometer lessons, each time thinking about the children in our room. I realize that if I follow these lessons as they are written, the children will not be engaged in the real work of science. A thermometer is a tool used to measure temperature; it is a tool a scientist uses for a purpose. The problem is that there *is* no authentic purpose for the student to use a thermometer in these lessons. Curiosity is an authentic reason, a compelling reason, to experiment, but following directions does not spark curiosity. Having time to explore sparks curiosity.

I ask myself, "How can a thermometer become a useful tool to a child scientist?" I think of the guide lesson where one child was directed to measure the temperature of a mixture of cold and hot water. Mixing water of different temperatures is interesting to adults and children. We adjust the faucets in the sink and shower until the water is our preferred temperature. I think about the children in our classroom. "What temperature water do you like to use when you wash your hands?" "Can you make water that temperature from the sink faucet?" "Can you use hot and cold water from these tubs to make the temperature you like?" I can see endless investigations and experiments that require the use of a thermometer. Children will begin watching to see how long it takes for the temperature of the water on one side of a container to change when water of a different temperature is poured into the other side. "How much should I add?" "What happens when I stir it?" More questions will arise, prompting still more experimentation. Replication of experiments occurs as experiments are shared. Procedures will be described and refined so that others can "try to do what Becky did."

## Side Effects

What are the side effects of such a hands-on approach to learning about weather and thermometers, or any other topic? The most harmful effect is that it trivializes the role of the child scientist. The child's role is limited to following directions. Investigations are set out for the child to follow step by step. The child makes no choices or decisions and is denied the opportunity to identify and solve science problems. This is "paint-by-number" science. Remember when paint-by-number was a popular activity for children and adults? A painting kit included a pre-printed map of a painting with areas outlined and identified by number. The "painter" then filled in each area with the corresponding premixed color and produced a "painting." I wonder, did the painter confront and solve the problems of an artist? Did the paint-by-number exercises teach the painter how an artist works, to learn more about art? Did the paint-by-number participants come to appreciate and understand the work and contributions of artists? How does paint-by-number science teach children to confront and solve the problems of science? Does it teach children how scientists work? Will children come to appreciate and understand the work and contributions of scientists? Will they become critical consumers of science?

## An Alternative to Lessons

Science need not come in "lessons." The following description of what we did with the weather kit shows another approach to introducing thermometers. The science kit is here. I have thirty-two small Celsius/Fahrenheit thermometers, numerous plastic cups, thirty-two hand lenses, a large collection of weather-related tradebooks, and the critical component—a room of first-grade kids.

We are gathered on the rug for science workshop. The children know from the day's plans that we will be using a thermometer. I give the children ten minutes to write what they already know about thermometers. None of the children has finished writing what they know, but they will have many opportunities to add to this entry in their science notebook. Everyone shares one thing they have written:

- There's numbers on a thermometer.
- You use it when you're sick.
- We have one outside the kitchen window.
- My mom uses a thermometer when she cooks turkey.
- My grandma uses a thermometer when she makes candy. Yummmm.
- There's red inside a kind of glass straw.
- It goes down when it's cold outside.
- We got one in the aquarium. It bounces up when you push it down.
- There's lots of lines all the way to the top.

I tell the class that we will be using thermometers and that these thermometers have what Karen described as a glass "straw." I add, "Not one of the first graders I have had in my room has ever broken a thermometer. But if a thermometer breaks, then someone should come and get me so that I can clean up the glass before anyone is cut." "Oh," I say, "one other reminder—"

"We know. It's science and nothing goes in your mouth—like a thermometer," comes the chorus.

I hand out the thermometers. A few children sit and study their thermometers, most scatter around the room.

After five minutes I call them back. We talk briefly about what they have done. I tell them that for the next ten minutes they need to write down what they do with the thermometer and what they notice. Off they go again. I watch as children place their thermometers under paper, in pockets, on the heater. A couple head for the coat room. Out come backpacks, mittens, coats, lunch boxes. "Remember to write what you do and what you notice," I tell them.

After ten minutes I call the class to a scientists' meeting. The children come with pencils, scientists' notebooks, and thermometers. There is so much excitement that I decide today we should just talk about what we did first, then talk about what we noticed, rather than talking about both together. We go around the circle glancing at notes and describing one thing we did. I hear many, "I'm going to try that" comments, so I give the class time to write plans for tomorrow in the back of their notebooks. (I know many of the children's plans will change after listening to others' observations, but I like the idea of listening and adding to plans as children hear from each other. Being able to add to and change plans develops a stance of openness—for changing plans and for new evidence. And hopefully for revision of explanations.) Everyone has calmed down and we reread our notes before we begin discussing things we noticed. I record their observations on a chart:

- The red line went up when I put my thumb on it.
- I took my book's temperature. (Laughter.) It was right on top of 70.
- Mine went down when I stuck it in the water fountain.
- My shirt pocket was one line up 70 and my pants pocket was two lines up. That's funny. My shirt's taller than my pants.
- I didn't draw all the little lines. Just the ones around the number where the red stopped. It's kinda hard to draw all those little lines.
- Inside my lunch box was the same as inside my backpack.
- The heater was under the 80 number. It was real close.
- My coat pocket was real close to 70.
- My thumb was 90. That's more than the heater.
- I didn't write how much, but my mitten was really hot.
- It went up when I blew on it. I didn't put it in my mouth, I just blew on it.

I ponder the children's comments. (I think that tomorrow we'll spend part of our time checking to see how many things we can find in our room that are the same temperature and think about why that could be.) Now I say, "Some of you used numbers when you shared your observations. Let's look closely at the numbers. What do you notice?"

- They go up by ten. More and more and more.
- Yeah, and they go down by ten—see, it keeps getting more when it goes down too. And when you hold it sideways, it gets ten more out from zero. It gets ten more both ways.

- There's lines in between every number.
- There's five lines in between every number.
- I think it's like a graph. You hold it like this and you count. And under it is what it's counting. I put it on the rug and the rug's temperature is just on top of 70—one line on top.

I stop here. What a wonderful connection—the scale on the thermometer and the scale on a graph. I explain that in between each ten the lines count by twos. "We haven't practiced counting by twos yet," I say, "but lots of things come in twos so we'll practice today during math time. Then it will be easier to count lines. Leave your thermometers on your table. You'll want to check the temperature during the day."

In one science period the children have had their hands on thermometers and some have begun to build an understanding of how thermometers work. This is more than students learn in three of the kit lessons. Think of the time we have saved for our own questions and investigations. Were there *real* problems to solve? Yes, for some children. Some grappled with "How do thermometers work? What is going on? What is getting measured?" Others were involved in unstructured exploration, not yet making any connections or asking questions. Today the need was to explore and collect observations. (I watched, listened, and collected information too, which will help me plan for tomorrow.) Today curiosity provided the need to measure temperature. Tomorrow, I know there will be other authentic needs. *Rigorous?* Yes. Tomorrow there will be disagreements about findings—disagreements that will be resolved by many readings of thermometers. I know enough about first grade scientists to know that in the coming weeks their plans and problems will frequently require the accurate reading of thermometers. Was the exploration *relevant*? Yes. The children were in control of their exploration. They decided how to use the thermometers.

Tomorrow comes, but not the way I had anticipated. Overnight the weather became bitterly cold for Maryland. When I arrive at school the temperature is 8°F. I know the children will come into school cold. This would be a perfect time to find out how cold it is, and to freeze water outside. I prepare cups for freezing water. (I label each cup with the child's name, and think about making a line on each cup so that I can measure an equal amount of water in each, but decide to have the children decide how much water they want. Then they would be sure to notice the difference in freezing time.) When the children come in they hurry to tables and pick up thermometers. Many are surprised that the room temperature is the same as yesterday. They feel cold and thought the temperature of the classroom would be lower. We talk about the cold weather, the puddles that had frozen from yesterday's rain, their cold faces and red noses. Just how cold is it outside?

We bundle up and go out. Even I am surprised at how quickly the red line dropped. It is 10°F. I pass out the cups. One child immediately blows into his. The condensation freezes on the inside of the cup. We all blow "dragon smoke" into our cups and scrape off the frozen water vapor. I pour water into cups, the children put in their thermometers, we leave the box on the frozen ground, and go inside. We check the cups thirty minutes later. Some cups of water are frozen. In an hour all are frozen. All but one thermometer shows 30°F, which is upside down and reads 10°F! Now we have a lot to talk about, and to figure out! We spend the morning thinking and talking about what had happened. "How could the air be colder than ice?" "What did the upside down thermometer measure?" "How come the top of the thermometer doesn't tell what the bottom does?" We observe our thermometers and melting water Popsicles™. Several children spend days investigating upside down thermometers. *Real? Relevant? Rigorous?* Yes.

## Making the Most of the Science Kit

At the beginning of this chapter I noted that science kits had come back to treat the ailments of science education in our schools. I expressed my hope that kits would help to provide an outstanding science program for our children, and my concern that there could be harmful side effects. I do not think we can afford a treatment that trivializes the role of the child scientist, and is patronizing and debilitating to teachers. We cannot have children spending time on lessons that are not real, relevant, and rigorous. Whatever the implications, science kits are here, they contain needed materials, and we can make them work for the children and for us.

I know the weather kit is coming and need a book of resources to go with it. As a first step, I'll get a large notebook, blank paper, and a three-hole punch. The weather unit will be the children's, but as their teacher I have the responsibility for preplanning. I began thinking about weather when I received the list of kits that would be coming to first-grade classrooms. I prepared a list of questions, and am sharing this list as I wrote it, not because it is a wonderful list, but because it is where I began—a list in progress. It begins with a couple of "getting warmed up and into the subject" questions, then moves to different weather topics. Some topics brought a flurry of questions, others I dropped after a single question. As I reread the list I realize that most of the questions are closely connected to events and experiences in the lives of the children in the rural community where I teach (real and relevant). If I were teaching in the urban Chapter I schools where I taught for many years, the list would be different. I would have questions about the rainbows in oily puddles or the collections of blown leaves and papers in one corner of the playground. Here is my first list of weather questions, curiosities, and possibilities.

Where is the science in weather?
What do kids think about when they think about weather? How does it
        connect to their lives? What will they want to know about?
What makes clouds different shapes—different colors?
And rainbows—they'll want to know about rainbows . . .
What is weather?
Where does our weather come from?
What makes wind blow, and stop?
Why is the wind sometimes steady, other times gusty, or absent?
How many ways can we make wind at school?
How about wind breakers: What fabrics break the wind? . . . trees as
        wind breakers . . . snow fences, sand dunes at the beach . . .
What do the kids know about air? Will they understand air pressure?
Wind direction—what difference does it make? Why does wind shift
        directions?
What evidence is there of wind force, and of wind direction—plants?
How do we measure wind? What are we measuring? What evidence of
        wind is on the kids' farms—soil erosion, paint on farm buildings?
What are connections of weather and farm, planting, harvesting, sun and
        rain, rain and soil? What causes rain drops to be different sizes?
        Why are some drops so big—others a drizzle?
What's in rain? Where does acid rain come from?
What evidence is around of condensation, evaporation? What difference
        does it make?
What kinds of fabrics are waterproof? How can we make fabrics
        waterproof—water repellant? (Absorb and repel as concepts—
        heat, water, light)

Temperature—when does it snow? How can it snow when the
        temperature is above freezing?
Freezing rain—why isn't it snow instead of freezing rain?
Ice—what makes it slippery? How cold is ice? Can ice ever get colder?
Think about snow as insulation—clothing insulation, building
        materials . . .
What do kids know about thermometers—scale, expansion, and
        contraction of liquids? Who made the first thermometer? How
        are thermometers made? (Think about scale, size, variety of
        thermometers.)
What tools do meteorologists use? Why? How developed? Who
        developed? How do they work?
What do scientists do when they study the weather? What interests them?
        What questions do they ask? What problems do they have?

These are questions to get me started; I add the children's questions as we
go along.
        Sometimes we don't know enough about a topic to even begin ask-
ing questions. Guides can be a starting point. They provide ideas to react
to and build upon. They can jump-start our thinking. What are the lessons
in the guide about? In this weather guide they are about wind, temperature, rain, and clouds. That is a place to start talking with other teachers.
When we all start talking about wind we soon have ideas, connections,
and questions to work with: wind power, windmills, sailboats, converting
wind energy to . . . , making wind, fans, cooling (does wind lower the temperature or just make you feel more comfortable?), wind and water, hurricanes, drying, evaporation, pushing, lifting, flying, planes, balloons,
leaves, seeds, dust . . . This kind of brainstorming opens us to the many
possible ways the children will want to explore wind. It doesn't mean we
will set up all of the lessons, but that we will be prepared to support the
wind scientists in our room with their explorations and investigations. It is
a mental preparation that helps us listen, question, and play with the children's and our own ideas.
        What will I do with this collection of questions and ideas? For
now I'll just put everything in the question section of my notebook. When
it gets closer to the time for the kit to arrive I'll read them over and sort
them out into categories. Some teachers may think in big ideas and categories from the beginning. The notebook must work for the individuals involved.

I am a book person, so I include a bibliography section in my resource book. A couple of weeks before the kit comes I take out my list of questions and begin gathering books related to weather. I begin with the usual search of weather-related words. I look under weather, climate, rain, snow, ice, precipitation, wind, tornadoes, hurricanes, air, meteorology, water cycle, temperature, thermometer, insulation, clouds, rainbow, balloons . . . I collect information, fiction, biography, poetry, and art books. I tell the class that soon we will be studying weather. They look for books with stories or illustrations where weather is important. The children add to our collection. (See appendix for a list of weather-related titles.) We all begin reading and talking about the books. As we read we look at illustrations through new eyes, noticing things we had missed before. By the time the kit arrives our awareness and interest in weather has increased—so has our knowledge, and our questions.

By this time I am thinking of many possibilities. I know the children and am able to anticipate some of the connections they will probably make. I start a "connections" section in the notebook. First I just jot down headings on sheets of paper—Liquids, Color, Waterproofing, Insulation. I make a section for materials we may need that do not come with the kit. I know the children will be interested in color—the color of the sky, clouds, rainbows—and so we will need prisms. Some children may want to separate colors. I'll think about what they will need for that. We will collect different kinds of thermometers. We may need a supply of balloons . . .

Now I am thinking of investigations, projects, activities we might like to try. Can we make our own thermometers? How about a windmill? I add a section for people resources—high school science students, meteorologists, and people who are affected by the weather. I list people who drive snowplows, engineers, farmers, mail carriers. Our primary team teachers meet once a week. We share our notebooks and get ideas from each other. We take apart the guide that came with the kit, and punch the pages with a three-hole punch, then rearrange it in a way that will work for us.

The resource book is growing, and will continue to grow all year. It contains more possibilities than we can ever investigate. It is comforting to know there is so much to work on, but there is still a big question. If we don't follow lessons from the guide, then exactly how will we work? What kind of structure will hold this together? I am comfortable with a workshop structure (see Reardon 1993). Our structure comes from the predictability of mini-lessons, use of our scientists' notebooks, exploration and investigation time, and scientists' meetings. Thinking about the structure used for math time or writing workshop or reading may be helpful for others. What is important is that we include enough time for children to investigate their own questions and solve their own problems within our framework. And that the weather kit, or any kit, does not control us, but works for the children and for us. We must have a workable structure in place before the kit arrives.

The kit arrives. The children are excited; we are excited. Let's open it together! Let's pour out the contents and think about how those materials were selected. What can we do with them?

I think of the weather kit that arrives in my room as free round trip plane tickets to Weatherland. To use these tickets I must take the whole class with me. The great thing is that once we get off the plane in Weatherland we can use and choose from the contents of the kit to travel wherever and however we choose. We don't have to stay together and do all of the same things, but we do have to meet regularly, keep records and share what we have seen, done, and figured out from our travels through Weatherland so far. Oh yes, as pilot and travel consultant, I have extra responsibilities: I must listen to all of the travelers, help organize the meetings, set an agenda, give mini lessons (about the language, customs, and features of the land), stimulate discussion, provoke and prompt questions, make available time and materials, schedule side trips, make connections, encourage the timid, set speed limits for the reckless, keep records . . .

As we read the guides that accompany kits we must think critically about the lessons presented. My experience is that many of the lessons are not wrong, but are irrelevant. Time is a scarce resource in our classrooms. When we throw out these irrelevant lessons we make time for the children's science. We must continually ask, "How is this activity relevant?" "Whose science is this?" "Is it rigorous?" "Would a scientist do that?" "Why are the children doing that—for whom?" "How does that help the child to become a scientist?" "Is there a reason for everyone to use that record form?" "Whose problem is this? Is it the child's problem?" "Can the children design their own way to solve that problem?" "How can we test that?" "When will we talk about this?" "What will the children plan to do next?"

The teacher's guide can never replace what we as teachers know about our children and about their progress in becoming scientists. I have heard many critics argue that most teachers want and need the guides that accompany science kits, math materials, and reading anthologies. These critics believe the guides have been written by experts who know the hierarchy of skills that must be mastered before children can proceed. If teachers do not follow the script of the guide, children will not master the skills. A few outstanding teachers can teach without following the guides, these critics say, but most teachers cannot. I strongly disagree. I believe teachers *are* able to analyze and plan for learning without scripted lessons. Learning science is not a step-by-step progression through a predetermined hierarchy of activities and skills. The guides are generic and not written for our class. We must not let the procedures and message of the guide distract our attention from what the child is doing and saying. Our best teaching will come from listening to and watching the children with their hands in science.

## Bibliography

National Science Resources Center. 1991. *Weather and Me: Field Test Edition*. Washington, DC: National Academy of Sciences.

National Science Resources Center. 1995. *Weather*. Washington, DC: National Academy of Sciences. (Published by Carolina Biological Supply Company, Burlington, NC.)

Reardon, J. 1993. "Developing a Community of Scientists." In *Science Workshop: A Whole Language Approach*, ed. W. Saul et al. Portsmouth, NH: Heinemann.

Westly, J. 1988. *Rocks, Sand, and Soil*. Sunnyvale, CA: Creative Publications (*Windows on Science*™).

# II

# What's Important?

# 3 Carole Roberts

# The Building Blocks of Science

I was a typical overwhelmed teacher when I first heard about The Elementary Science Integration Project (ESIP). ESIP was designed for teachers interested in integrating hands-on science with writing, reading, and other curricular areas. I hoped I had finally found the solution to the problem of how to do more in what seemed to be shorter and shorter school days. Instead, I found myself grappling with even greater issues. The following excerpts from my daily journal show how my experience helped me analyze and rebuild my classroom to better meet my needs and those of my students.

**July 7, 1992** Two days into ESIP and I'm feeling very inadequate. I have heard so many ideas about what makes up a good classroom and many are unfamiliar. All of them seem to involve giving the children choices—choices of what they will read or what they wish to investigate in science. I realize my school system is not supporting hands-on, integrated methods of teaching. The goals and policies of the school system are moving toward process rather than product, but the needed material support and training is missing.

A new first-grade teacher who understands and loves science and whole language joined our school staff this year. It was an extra plus to see her child-centered classroom. I see it as a chance for some of my kids to find greater opportunities to grow and learn for themselves next year.

How refreshing it is to walk into her classroom and see a room much like my own with clusters of desks where children can talk and discuss their work. Choices abound, whether it be the books children read or the art projects they undertake. The daily plans are a loose story, not blocks of time. The subject areas are woven together and there is an interrelatedness to it all. Yes, there are some worksheets, but they are carefully used. They require writing and reading and experimenting rather than filling in the blanks. In this room science isn't taught just twice a week—it's a daily presence. It is not taught from a kit or a textbook, but from real things that interest first graders.

Can two people in a school make a difference? Listening to other ESIP teachers, it sounds like schools that have had success with integrated, hands-on programs have a consensus among staff and a real commitment to early childhood education. Our school is curriculum- and book-driven. Our inservice programs stress how to implement the new curriculum rather than discuss general strategies for teaching. Maybe that's what I'm most uncomfortable with. How can a classroom be child-centered when someone is saying exactly what, how, and when the children should learn?

## July 8, 1992

Yesterday as I drove home I thought more about why I was feeling so frustrated. I realized that I had learned the function of kindergarten, or any grade, was to get kids ready for the next grade. I should give children the skills and behaviors needed to succeed in future years. If I did not do this I was setting them up for failure. That's not what I learned in my early childhood program, but it was the expectation of the principal and parents. I had reached a happy compromise where I was comfortable, the administration was comfortable, the parents were comfortable, and most of the kids were comfortable, too. My program wasn't bad, but it could be better.

The ideas presented in ESIP so far have reminded me how much I have strayed from a child-centered classroom. I yearn to try out some of these ideas, but part of me is saying, "What justice will it do if I give the children something so different from what they will experience in first grade and beyond?" I have come to see my classroom as a bridge that children cross to move into the real world of school. I worry that this bridge will not be extended by the first grade, that it will be culture shock for my students. How will they go from choices to no choices? Right now I give them a mixture of both to help them adjust.

My gut feeling is to let the room become their classroom. I realize I have been moving toward this over the years—giving them more and more of the decision making and responsibility. But will the adjustment be too hard next year? Will it work if I only worry about myself and what I feel is best for the children? If I let the other teachers be a bit more uncomfortable next year might this encourage *them* to change or will our good relationship dissolve? I've seen that happen in other schools where the teachers demand that upcoming children do things the previous teacher felt were inappropriate. Will my kids be overwhelmed and frustrated?

Someone said today that the hard thing about inquiry is that we're crossing lines and letting children set the boundaries. This will surely be difficult for teachers. Traditional teaching has the teacher in control. Many teachers and administrators expect chaos or off-task behavior if that control is relinquished.

## July 16, 1992

I found today's discussion about going beyond hands-on science to inquiry very thought provoking. Science kits take the present curriculum and put the materials in the children's hands, then allow the children to carry out the demonstrations that were once done for them. Although hands-on science takes a step forward from teacher demonstrations, the children still are not learning what scientists really do. Children should, like scientists, formulate a question and experiment or research to find an answer. No wonder children aren't doing better in science or choosing scientific fields for their occupations. The essence that science can be fun, a bit like a mystery, an enjoyable pursuit, is lost. It is lost when we tell them exactly what we expect them to do and discover.

The importance of perseverance was also mentioned today. This means we must give the children *time* to persist. I often say, "I need everyone to join me for this story or lesson," and demand that all the kids stop and join me. Next year I plan to be more aware that children sometimes need to go on beyond the time limits I've set. They need the freedom to keep exploring the next day.

I felt very overwhelmed after the second presentation today. The message was good, but it was the last block I had to balance on my mental structure of a good classroom. (Being a kindergarten teacher I was visualizing a tower that consisted of all the things I felt were important to my program, and I was piling on all the new ideas I learned through ESIP.)

This last idea was just too much for the structure to bear. It all came tumbling down! I'm not distraught right now, just weary. Lying on the floor are scattered blocks, many of them new to me—inquiry science, book clubs, science boxes, alternate assessments, reading workshop, and teaching through children's questions. Strewn among them are the things I was worrying my way through last year—cooperative learning, writer's workshop, and our new math curriculum. Of course there are things still there from my old comfort zone, but now I'm even questioning those. Wendy's been asking for questions all week; my biggest ones now are, "How do I rebuild a better stronger tower? How do I convince myself and the parents it was worth the change?"

I'm not sure where to begin, but surprisingly I feel very calm about it right now. I realize I may have to eliminate or modify some of my blocks to make this work for me. I may even have to leave a few blocks out of my tower. I have some ideas starting to brew now, and luckily I'll have August to work through them before school begins. It's exciting, yet scary. How do I explain and justify such a big change? It's as if I am admitting that what I thought I was doing right all this time is wrong. All I can say is that it's what is best for the children. I hope that's enough.

I'd like to start next year with a theme. I don't normally do themes but this one may help me tie all the "new stuff" together. The theme will be "Welcome to a World of Wonder." I'd like to do *wonder charts* throughout the year, beginning with *What Do You Wonder About Kindergarten?* I think the kids probably have a lot of questions about kindergarten. I could use similar charts for content areas: What Do You Wonder About Magnets? What Do You Wonder About Books?

I'd also like to make up something called a Wonder Circle. We'd take an idea off the wonder chart or have a child tell something she wondered about. Then we'll go around the circle and discuss that question. This will help me see what the children know, what misinformation they have, and will nurture a sharing of ideas.

I also want to incorporate science boxes (exploration boxes filled with materials on a topic) into my classroom. If I base them on our curriculum topics I can allow for free inquiry and cover the required science curriculum. Our curriculum includes the five senses, plants, magnets, and animals. Surely, I can make some boxes that allow the children to further explore these topics.

Boy, if I had all day kindergarten this might be easier. I feel stressed for time. Someone recently pointed out that if I was feeling stressed the children probably were, too. It reminded me that the times I really saw inquiry coming out in my room were with my most difficult class. I was so burned out I just said, "I'm tired of breaking my back trying to get all this in. These kids need to be kids and I just need to spend some time playing with them." I had the answer then, but the pressure to do what's expected, and the habits of many years, would not allow that revelation through.

My biggest concern now is whether I have the energy it will take to change my classroom so much, and whether I have the strength to worry my way through it. In the past I had some sense of how my children would act and how to guide them through. Now I feel like I am entering unfamiliar territory. Maybe if I saw a two-session kindergarten teacher doing reader's workshop and inquiry science. . . . I know I would still have to worry through it to find how it best works for me, but to see someone who feels comfortable with it would be helpful. . . . I still have some doubts as to how some of this will work with very young children.

## July 17, 1992

"One room, two classes" kept running through my head as I left ESIP today. Maybe I have found something in common with middle school teachers. When I envision a "child-centered classroom" I envision a place where projects get started and often are carried on through another day. I envision lots of materials, some of which will be left out overnight— or for days. How to keep little hands from disturbing these things? (I know, it should start to build respect!) Where will I find space for fifty kids who share the room over a six hour period? Oh, well, one more thing to worry through. (After two weeks of intensive learning and exchanging of ideas, we had a breather—a week off—before returning for one more week of the ESIP Summer Institute.)

## July 25, 1992

I haven't done much serious thinking during this week off. School seems so far away and I don't want to make many plans until I can meet my kids and feel my way through all this. I'm afraid if I start working things out too much I'll be frustrated by reality. I do know my first block in rebuilding my tower will be the children. They will be the foundation I build from.

**July 28, 1992**    A lot of people are saying they can't wait to get back to school and start working on their ESIP projects. They are so excited and confident. ESIP must really click with their present program and school. I'm scared! I don't know why because I've always had the confidence that I could explain things to parents and administrators, knowing they would trust me and support me. Maybe it's because of how much our school system stresses its curriculum. The message is that curriculum is the most important thing for the teacher to focus on. On back to school night we must talk about "the curriculum." Early in the school year we must sit down and prepare long range plans that show how we are going to present all of the objectives in "the curriculum." A copy of the long range plan goes to the area office so they know we are following "the curriculum." When we are observed for evaluations, we must have objectives in our lesson plan that come from "the curriculum." Some principals even require that the objectives from "the curriculum" be posted daily in the classroom. We're not teachers, we're curriculum presenters! We've lost sight of what is really important—the children. I'm going to write myself a message and put it above my desk next year, FOR THE CHILDREN. Sometimes I lose sight of that. Eight years ago my attitude was the one ESIP is trying to develop, but I lost a lot of that. In trying to be a team player, in trying to give new things a chance, I lost sight of what I really believed.

Someone commented to me that people only change when they are ready. I wonder if that's why I'm having a harder time with ESIP than so many others. Maybe they are only hearing what they want to hear? Either they don't feel uncomfortable right now, or they filter out things that might cause conflict. Me, I'm taking it all in and grappling with it.

**September 1992**    I feel pretty good about how things are going in my classroom. I'm reminding myself that Rome wasn't built in a day, and doing my best to bring questions and wonder into our class. We have done two wonder charts. It was interesting to look at the "wonders" children had about kindergarten. I could see a lot of background knowledge come out in their questions. I could tell that they were using observations to make inferences and show excitement about what we might be doing this year— "Are we going to do this?"

Using the words "What do you wonder about . . . ?" helped the children formulate *questions* instead of telling stories or sharing things they already knew. If they made a statement I gently reminded them that a question was something they didn't know the answer to yet. After two weeks of observing monarch caterpillars, eggs, and chrysalises we did another wonder chart. Wow! The kids had super questions! They asked me if I was going to give them the answers. I told them that like their wonders about kindergarten, they would find out the answers to these questions as we watched the monarchs, read books, and watched movies. As the weeks passed we reviewed the chart and added answers. Sometimes the kids would say, "Hey, that was one of our questions. Let's write the answer."

But the questions are just the starting place. I realize that there is a lot more involved in nurturing a sense of wonder. First, it is important that the children get lots of experience manipulating real things. They also need *time* to explore. I'm adapting my lessons to involve more partner and small group activities rather than keeping the whole class together. I gave each small group a caterpillar to observe crawling around on a piece of paper. What an experience for the children! I put the caterpillars in smaller, unbreakable containers before they made chrysalises and then placed one on each table for part of the day.

I find that I'm often going to libraries to get books on the subjects we are studying. I realize that I can make my classroom more child-centered without ignoring the curriculum. By starting with questions, I am showing the children that I value what they wonder about the required topic. I realize everything doesn't have to be self-chosen in a child-centered classroom. It is important that I hear their voices within the limits that need to be imposed.

I'm also trying to build a risk-taking atmosphere. This is taking some flexibility on my part. Some days I have to just let things go, and not worry that I haven't accomplished everything I had planned. Sometimes I have to bite my lip and let children be somewhere they aren't supposed to be as long as they are truly engrossed in what they are doing and safety is not an issue.

## October 1992

The other day the children were making paper models of the life cycle of the monarch butterfly. A child asked if she could get the cage so that she could make hers look like the real one. The conversation at that table was so fascinating I grabbed a piece of paper and started writing. Not only were the children using appropriate vocabulary, but they were having a discussion about whether it was a "male" or "female" butterfly that had just "emerged." That day some of the children added scent glands to their models; others left them off because they wanted theirs to be girls.

**November 1992**    We went on a leaf hunt a few days ago. I told the children I wanted them each to be sure to bring back five leaves, and they all had to be different either in shape or color. That was a challenge! We didn't do a wonder chart. Now I wish I had because the kids just didn't get as interested in finding out more about leaves. There was one really exciting exchange. Michael was making some rubbings from leaves that I had preserved in contact paper. He asked me what kind of leaf one of them was. I suggested we look in some of the reference books I had picked up at the library. He took one book, I took the other and we searched through them, stopping now and then to get each other's opinion. This leaf did not seem to be in any of the books.

Then I asked if maybe he had left a part off when he did the rubbing. He got the leaf he had rubbed, but it looked the same to us. I told Michael that my first thought was that maybe it was a mutant leaf, one that was just different from all the others under the tree. I told Michael I had found a match for each leaf, so there had to be others like it under the tree. He found the match in the box. Robbie offered to bring in his leaf book and Michael said he would check the public library. We never did find the exact leaf in a book, but the experience was much more important than the answer. How important is it that we find the answers? The process is more important, I think.

**December 1992**    Things have slowed down with the holidays coming. I just haven't had time, or found any subject matter that really excites the children. What can I do? I need to find something that the kids can really get their hands into.

**January 1993**    Snow! High interest, that's for sure! When my afternoon class arrived today I sent three children out to fill containers with snow. As the trays sat on the table I asked the kids to tell me what "Snow is . . ." This was our first attempt at the K part of the KWL chart (What I *Know*, *Won*der about, and *Learned*). Quickly we came up with an excellent list of observations. Next we passed the snow dishes around. The children had time to further explore the snow. I noticed some of them were verifying things others had said and pointed this out. They began making new observations that we added to the chart. They noticed that the snow in some of the containers was more melted than in the others. They began to talk excitedly about why this was so. Later I read *Snow Is Falling*, a "Let's Find Out" book by Franklyn Branley. We put thermometers in the trays and looked at the temperature. We sang some songs about snowmen. The kids seemed so interested. Yet, their interest melted as the snow did. On to something else.

## February 1993

I tried to audiotape the children's science conversations and then get them transcribed. How frustrating! ESIP offered to help me find someone to write down what the children were saying as they worked with science materials. This helped because Joanne wrote little side notes that told what the kids were doing as they talked. I still don't feel like I'm getting what I need from this. Maybe it's because I want to be there myself. When I have time to see and watch I see so much. I can tell what children are thinking when they experiment. I can hear things in their voices.

The kids have been observing the way water changes things. This was a topic that sprang from our five senses unit. I set up a chart on the bulletin board with the heading "How does the texture change when something is put in water?" with six things the children had to try, then they could experiment with anything else they selected. I found time to meet with each group and record their observations. It was fun to go over to the table and model, "I wonder what happened to the sugar cube you put in?" and watch their eyes widen when they realized it wasn't there anymore. They would ask for another cube and watch it disappear. On another day I was able to relate how a sponge expands in water to what happens to croutons when they are placed in water. Wow! There really is a sense of wonder developing here. I'm as excited about this as the kids.

## March 1993

Our *Scholastic Let's Find Out* magazine had a unit on volcanoes. I probably wouldn't have worked with something so abstract except I couldn't throw out four magazines. We did the little experiment and read the little articles. The kids were so excited by it that I went to the public library and checked out some books. They were literally hiding them from each other and fighting over them. They asked our school librarian for volcano books. A child in one class brought in real volcanic ash and pumice from Mount St. Helens. Some children wrote their own little books about volcanoes. It's becoming *their* classroom. I can do this!

### Early April 1993

It was time to start our plants and seeds unit. This time I asked the children to go around the circle and tell something they knew about plants or ask a question. We had a good mix and children learned from each other. This science community is really building.

### Late April 1993

The plants have done very well. The children saw the need for water and sunlight after one weekend when some plants withered and others were stretched toward the window. The ones under the PTA's growth light were growing straight and tall and were not as dry as those on the heater. Some of the ones under the twenty-four-hour growth lamp even touched the light!

I found an onion at the store that had roots and stuck it in some water. It sprouted more roots and then a luscious green stem. It became a daily ritual for some of the students to rush back to the shelf to see how much it had grown. Sitting in a juice can, the bulb grew smaller as the plant used its food. Eventually it fell into the water, no longer able to be held by the can. Gosh, this sure beats the old dry lessons on the parts of a plant and what plants need.

### May 1993

The year is almost over. Our last wonder chart is about the chicken eggs we are hatching. After a couple of weeks of reading books about hatching eggs and candling the eggs I ask if the children have any questions. As usual, questions abound.

What a different atmosphere from my former classrooms! Every day the children run to the science area the moment they come in the door. I've moved my science area from the back wall to a more central location closer to the meeting rug. Children have appointed themselves observers in order to keep the class up to date on what is happening. The whole class gathers around. I'm finding that sometimes I must call children away because they are not getting other assignments done.

When we have a guest speaker my students never once go off on a tangent or start telling stories. They ask intelligent questions. The speakers are impressed: "How old did you say these children are?"

I'm constantly having books pushed in my face and being asked questions—"How old is this chick embryo, Mrs. Roberts?" I have to suggest that maybe the two children wrestling over a science book could sit down and look at it together. The children are writing and talking more about what they have learned.

I am very pleased with what developed in my classroom. Over the year I didn't accomplish everything I wanted to, but I did my best. I had to forget about by-the-book cooperative learning lessons, social settings, and making science boxes. By no means am I comfortable with what I've done, but my block tower is growing. Now I feel like my children's voices are being heard as well as mine. I hope my students felt I cared about what they wondered. It's no longer just my agenda being followed, but ours.

## Bibliography

Branley, F.M. 1986. *Snow Is Falling*. New York: Harper & Row.

*Scholastic Let's Find Out* 27, no. 6 (March 1993).

# 4  Debra Bunn

# "There's a Squid in Mrs. Bunn's Classroom!"

Peals of laughter, whispers, and an occasional "yech!" and "eeeww!" echoed in the hallways as word spread among the students. Today was the day and curiosity levels were high. Pleas of "Can we see them now, Mrs. Bunn?" and hasty offers—"Can I help give them out, Mrs. Bunn?"—rang out as students quickly dropped their winter outdoor garb and bookbags in a trail leading to my desk. Taking a quick glance at the clock, I made a pitch to reestablish the classroom routine of lining up outside the classroom door to wait for the morning bell. "I'm sure if you get your things put away, and you're standing in line quietly, you'll be asked to help me." No sooner said than done—the classroom cleared out!

What, you're probably wondering, could possibly get this motley crew of students to react so swiftly and cohesively? As one frustrated second-grade student told his teacher as he was ordered out of the fifth-grade line, "But there's a *squid* in Mrs. Bunn's classroom!" His teacher just looked at me, shook her head, and said resignedly, "Please make sure your door is closed today, Mrs. Bunn." The reason behind her request was not that my students were too *noisy* (although they often were), but that other students were too *nosy*! This had happened before—other students on restroom breaks would find their way into my classroom during science and would begin working on a project with my class before I even discovered them. Most of the teachers in our small school knew that if their kids didn't return right away, then more than likely they could be found in my room doing science.

I viewed the children's attraction and intense involvement as a much longed-for prize. This was what I had worked toward since the beginning. A way to teach that would stimulate and nurture my students' imagination in science.

## The Diversity of the Class

My first teaching assignment was a fifth grade at a public K–6 elementary school located on a military base in Maryland. About 80 percent of the students were military dependents and the remaining 20 percent were children from nearby civilian communities and a homeless shelter. With the average stay of the military dependents being three years, the homeless students averaging an eighteen-month stay, and the few civilian children constantly having to make new friends, this was a highly transient, fragmented population. Racially, the school was about half white and the other half a mixture of African-Americans, Asians, Native Americans, and Hispanics. Over half of the students qualified for reduced or free lunches.

With such social, economic, and cultural diversity came many rewards. Children were able to share widely varying traditions, languages, values, and perspectives with one another. Nevertheless, there were two major problems inherent in this setup: 1) inconsistencies in prior academic skills and knowledge, and 2) difficulties in developing working relationships with classmates. When I first read the cumulative records of my students, I was amazed at the disparity in curriculum between Maryland and other states, and the United States and other countries. Occasionally, I would get the non-English version of a student's record and then hope that an English version would follow, or that someone could translate it for me. It was incumbent upon me to find a way to quickly establish an environment in which there was a common base of knowledge and skills, and a cohesive community of learners.

## The First Year: "I Hate Science. I Can't Do It!"

My first year of teaching was difficult, but it was made even more horrendous as I discovered that I was teaching science exactly as I had been taught in elementary school. Although I could remember little about my childhood experiences with science, what I did recall was negative. Experimentation was teacher-directed, and had to be done exactly the way the instructor wanted it done. I hated that! Why was it wrong to want to do something based on what I wanted to know? However, most often the teacher performed the experiments while we, the students, watched. I remember thinking that our textbooks had been written by someone who enjoyed boring and confusing us. Teachers expected us to memorize what often couldn't be understood. The routine: read a chapter, review the chapter, and be tested on the chapter. I remember the sepia-toned science films in which the scientist, always a white male, would speak in an agonizingly monotonous voice. It was difficult for me to identify with this model of a scientist. If you had told me then that female and minority scientists existed, I wouldn't have believed you. Nonetheless, we were all equal in one respect; anyone could court big trouble by asking questions the teacher couldn't answer. It's no wonder that I avoided taking science as much as possible in high school and college.

Looking back at my first year as a teacher, I realized that I had been teaching as I had been taught. I used the curriculum guide like a Bible—adhering to it religiously unit by unit, filmstrip by filmstrip, and activity by activity. I assigned science vocabulary words, chapter readings, and end-of-chapter review questions. Then I tested my students on vocabulary, reading comprehension, and their ability to do multiple-choice tests. The ones who could not learn in this manner received low grades. During a conference with a student about her failing marks in science she said in a hopeless voice, "I hate science. It's boring. It's too hard, and I can't do it!" She complained about there being too much to read, and her inability to remember everything. I knew I had failed to make science better. I was frustrated—I wanted my students to enjoy science, but I didn't know how to make it meaningful to them. They were interested in science phenomena—their constant questioning about falling leaves, green bugs, and snowflakes attested to that fact. But their needs as learners, and let's face it, my needs as a teacher, could not be met by simply following the impersonal dictates of science curriculum guides with their recipe formats.

Then the science kits arrived and they seemed like a gift! The kits provided opportunities for application of knowledge and skills. Using a kit to teach my students about rocks and minerals was fine for basic skills. They used chemicals to test the composition of rocks, and learned how to break rocks using hammers and chisels. And the experiments in the workbooks, often preceded by workbook questions, were easy to follow. However, I found it difficult to keep my students on the assigned tasks. First, they put acids on the wrong rocks. Then, they brought in rocks they found outside the classroom and wanted to perform tests on them. They dropped rocks into the fish tank. The final straw occurred when one put the acid solution on pencils, plastic rulers, and leaves. What was going on here? What were they thinking? Why did they stray from the workbook's activities? I failed to find answers to those questions that term. Instead, the year ended with me feeling that I had failed the students. My enthusiasm for teaching was decimated, and I felt I needed out of the classroom.

## "Debra, Got Any Plans for the Summer?"

Anticipating a lazy, long period of rest before having to face another depressing year of teaching, I received a phone call from Dr. Wendy Saul in the education department at the University of Maryland Baltimore County, a friend with an uncanny ability for reading people. "Debra, got any plans for the summer?" she asked. I started to assure her that I did, but she would know if I were lying, and besides, I detected suppressed excitement in her voice. "No, not really," I replied hesitantly, all the time wondering what I was getting myself into. Wendy's reply: "Great! Have I got something for you."

The "something" was the Elementary Science Integration Project (ESIP), a two-year teacher research program involving the integration of science and literature. Would I like to participate as a novice teacher? My quick response—"What do I have to do?"

Reflect on what science is like in your classroom, she told me. I could do that. Maybe a summer with experienced teachers would give me some better ideas about teaching science, and motivating children to learn.

## The "Big Question"

I was intimidated at first by the high caliber of teachers selected for the program—teachers who had won prestigious awards, who possessed years of experience, and who were authors themselves. I felt handicapped by a lack of professional development, only one year's teaching experience, and a quirky personality, and was worried that I wouldn't fit in. Eventually, I discovered that ESIP allowed a diverse group of teachers to form a community of researchers. It didn't matter if the teacher was experienced, preservice, or a novice, because we all had questions about teaching. As I listened to those clearly able teachers questioning their own techniques, philosophies, and abilities, a light bulb or two lit inside my head and I began looking at my trials and tribulations in the classroom in a different way. What would happen if I changed my approach to science? How could I move from textbook science to inquiry science? It was a period of discovery as I participated in journal writing, discussion groups, and an exploration of open-ended hands-on activities.

At the end of the summer session, we were asked to state what "big question" we were going to research over the school year. My discussion group had said earlier that my question, "How can I make my students like science?" was too big. I needed to pinpoint a specific aspect, but I just couldn't get beyond that general question. How could I settle on any *one* thing to change when I felt that I needed to change *everything*? I decided to change my approach. How do you know when people like something? They become involved in the doing of it. If you like to read, you read. If you like to play sports, you play sports. And if you like science, you do science. Ergo, it stands to reason that if my students like science, they will do science. Aha! That was my big question: *How do you get students to want to do more science?* What is it about science that kids enjoy most?

My mind was in a turmoil as I thought back to the science activities we had done over the past year. For the unit on astronomy, we made astrolabes, we did cut and paste models of the planets, and we did an activity where one child was the sun and nine others were the planets revolving around it. For the unit on animals and animal adaptations we made a cut and paste booklet of the frog's life cycle, and a multitude of reports on assigned animals. Throw in a few filmstrips, videos, and word search puzzles and you have a picture of science in my classroom: boring, unimaginative, and narrowly focused. I resolved to change my attitude about science so that I could change my approach to it.

## "It's Ugly. It's Weird."

Since there was still time left in the summer, I decided I needed to do more science myself. I enrolled in the Baltimore Aquarium's Marine Biology workshop and for the next five days saw a side of science I couldn't believe existed. I steered a crab boat through the sunlit waves of the Chesapeake Bay, inched along a catwalk suspended over an open tank of deadly sharks, and dried and pressed a variety of seaweed. But for me the highlight of the week was the squid dissection. I had never seen a squid before—in person or in pictures.

When my partner and I were handed our specimen, I took one

look into the pan and jumped up out of my seat with a scream. The instructor rushed over to find out what had happened. I pointed at the pan and asked, "Is it alive?" She assured me that it wasn't and gently pressed me back into my chair. "If you don't feel you can do the dissection, just watch and take notes for you and your partner," she suggested.

I was thoroughly embarrassed by my behavior and tried to get back some modicum of composure. My partner, an old hand at dissections and a Maryland native, agreed to the instructor's suggestion. I watched, fascinated by the squid's physical appearance. The stringy tentacles with all those tiny little suckers. Did the suckers draw blood out of enemies? Was it a vampire of the ocean? Why were its eyes so big? I drew closer to the pan to more carefully observe the squid. What are those dots on its skin? Look at how colorful they are! I wanted my partner to hurry up on some things, and slow down on others. I decided to poke it with my finger. After all it was dead, and it couldn't hurt me. It felt cold, wet, and slimy. Ick! That was as far as I wanted to go that day with the squid.

During discussion I was asked what I thought about the squid. Dazed by the existence of such a creature, I replied, "It's ugly. It's weird. It's the neatest thing I've ever seen." Could they exist in fresh water? If they couldn't, why not? How would they react to differences in water temperatures? What effect would different types of light sources have on them? Would differences in diet have an impact on their behavior? My mind was racing with questions, questions that couldn't be answered with a few handouts, or in just one hands-on activity.

After the dissections, a few people cut up the squid's mantle into little rings, coated them with batter, and fried them in oil. I couldn't bring myself to eat one then, but I knew I would one day because this was not over. That evening I shared with my husband, a Maryland native, my experience with the squid. Wouldn't it be neat if I could do this in the classroom with my kids? My imagination was working overtime. I was seeing images of myself doing squid experiments, giant squid attacking ships, and someday being the expert on squid.

While I had been both repulsed and attracted to the squid, hours later I was still wound up from the whole experience. I had many questions, and I wanted answers. In reflecting on the experience I realized that my curiosity and imagination about the squid had made me like science, and wondered if my students would feel this same driving need to make discoveries about this unusual animal. I stayed up far into the night planning how I could slip the squid into a science unit on aquatic animals.

## I've Got to Nurture Their Imagination

The first week of school I didn't teach science. The combination of Maryland's new performance assessment tests, a renewed emphasis on accountability, and my lack of confidence in my new approach to teaching science had put me in a turmoil over what to do. I felt pressure to use the new science kits and to be successful in doing so. During the first semester I ended up teaching my science units straight from the textbook instead of the kits. This was fine for basic skills, but the classroom situation ended up being a repeat of the previous year—low grades, low participation, and numerous behavior problems.

Over the winter break I ran across an inspirational quote from Albert Einstein: "Imagination is more important than knowledge." What did the world's most celebrated and knowledgeable scientist mean? Was he intimating that imagination was a highly valued mental ability not in just the fine arts world, but also in the realm of test tubes and quantitative measurements? That maybe if I nurtured and stimulated my students' imagination they might become more involved in science? I resolved to begin treating children like scientists, by valuing their ideas, questions, and discoveries. I'm not going to be the teacher, I thought. Instead, I'll take the role of facilitator, and let them decide when and how I can help them. They'll see me in a different role, as a fellow learner who asks authentic questions and who accepts their answers and suggestions in my own investigations. If they know they are valued they may be more comfortable with allowing their imagination to lead them into original and creative explorations. I spent the rest of the break collecting everything I could find on squid and other ocean animals, blew the dust off the plans for squid investigations, and decided to risk trying something new.

## Doing What Scientists Do

"What is a scientist?" I asked my students as we huddled together for discussion time on the first day of the second semester. It was important that the children could identify scientists as people who asked a lot of questions. We read two books, *What Will Happen If . . . Young Children and the Scientific Method* by Barbara Sprung, and *How to Think Like a Scientist: Answering Questions by the Scientific Method* by Stephen P. Kramer, and we discussed our thoughts about scientists and the scientific method. I continued using the science kits, but this time I worked more on allowing the students to explore, generating a list of questions and hypotheses, and finding resources to help us discover answers. I practiced not jumping in with quick answers and solutions, but rather letting the students discover what they needed. Sometimes I provided an answer when it was needed to continue on with an experiment, but not when it was going to solve the mystery.

It was now the second week of the semester, and I was ready to stimulate their imagination. I dressed up in a yellow rain slicker, darkened the room, and lit a lone candle. The scene was set for my reading of a fifteenth-century ancient mariner account of the mythological Kraken, a giant squid. It supposedly attacked ships and pulled them down to the bottom of the sea. I asked the children if they thought there really were sea monsters like the Kraken. Most of the students said no, until I read them a true story of a giant squid attacking a fishing ship in the early 19th century. One of the crew members hacked off a portion of a tentacle that was later given to scientists to investigate. I asked, "What do we know about the Kraken? As scientists, how would you go about answering that question?" I then set up a scenario: while we couldn't sail out to sea and capture a giant squid, we could examine and dissect small ones in our classroom.

Since we were using plastic knives as scalpels, and the squid had been purchased from a local grocery store, I encountered no objection from the principal. With administrative approval behind us, we jumped into the scientific process. I instructed my students to act like scientists. The first thing they began to do was to ask questions about the squid.

I wonder if when they shoot their ink do they pollute (the water)?
Does it lay eggs or have birth like mammals?
Do they have brains?
Where do they get the black ink from?
Do they have teeth?
If they lost an arm would it grow back?
Why do they change colors when you freeze them?
What does a squid's heart look like?
How do they refill their ink sacs?
How fast do they swim?

I was impressed with the level and depth of thinking, and involvement evident during this period. We donned our aprons (plastic bags with holes cut out for head and arms) and began our activity. Many of the children had not seen a squid before and were very reluctant to touch it. I had a flashback to my own queasy first encounter, and shared it with them. It was assuring to them to know that I could be fearful of new experiences, too. They knew they didn't have to touch the squid if they didn't really want to, and that they could still be active participants. After the initial shock wore off, my students began examining the squid. As I wandered about the room I heard enthusiastic calls for my attention from children eager to share their discoveries.

"We cut it open and we had these. It looked like little eggs."
"Yeah, we think ours is a female."
"We looked in a book, and the book says they have about 2,000 eggs inside of them. And we decided there were about that many in there."
"It feels like a snail . . . because it's slimy and smooth."

## Stimulating and Nurturing the Imagination

The dissection of the squid opened doors for expansion into other areas of investigation. I extended the squid activity by adding on art activities such as squid printing. We fried squid rings, as I had done in my summer workshop, and this time I did try one. We all agreed with the student who pointed out that they "taste like chicken."

As the year progressed, the children continued to bring in information about the squid and its habitat. They also made connections between the squid and other aquatic animals and their biomes. This meant we covered more concepts than those listed in the curriculum guide. Testing changed from multiple choice to open-ended writing and performance assessments. My students' creative writing came to reflect what they knew about the subject.

## What I've Learned

At the end of the school year, I made a discovery. Not only did the children enjoy science, but I had developed a passion for teaching science. It was a far cry from the mind-dulling experience of the previous year, and from what I remembered from my own school experiences. Curriculum activities, kits, and filmstrips were still useful, but they were no longer the ruler by which I measured our ability to construct meaning out of phenomena. We had instead created a classroom where experimentation and questions were encouraged. By focusing on the use of our imagination, both the children and I were able to see science in a different light. Science became more meaningful when the children were granted the opportunity to personalize what they were learning, and I allowed myself to become a co-learner with my students.

Now, when my students walk into my classroom, faces beaming, eager to get started on their science inquiries, I feel that I have achieved my goal.

## Bibliography

Kramer, S.P. 1987. *How to Think Like a Scientist: Answering Questions by the Scientific Method.* New York: HarperCollins.

Sprung, B. 1985. *What Will Happen If . . . Young Children and the Scientific Method.* New York: Educ. Equity Concepts, Inc.

# 5 Linda Davis

# The Reason for Reasoning

We teach science when we help children think like scientists. While I am not the "official" science teacher in my school, I believe that I teach science when I help children use the kind of reasoning we use in science. This chapter describes the problem-solving processes we use in our classrooms—across the curriculum, and throughout the day.

**Watching Birds**  One Sunday last spring, I sat at my dining room table planning for the next week of teaching second grade. Stacks of papers and books surrounded me. In the middle of the afternoon, my husband suggested that I join him for a hike. I welcomed the idea and pulled on my sneakers.

We hiked along the edge of a wooded area nearby. Sunlight filtered through oak branches. A bird flew over our heads, emitting a nasal call. As it landed in a nearby tree, my husband watched its flight. "I can't tell if that's an adult or juvenile crow," my husband commented, squinting up at the bird. "It looks like an adult, but it sounds like a baby. Could you reach in my backpack and get out the binoculars?"

I unzipped his backpack and handed the binoculars to him.

After looking at the bird for about a minute, he said, "I think it's a juvenile. Here. Take a look and see what you think." He gave the binoculars to me.

Ordinarily this conversation would have passed unnoticed as typical of a hike with my naturalist husband. On this particular afternoon, though, I noticed that our brief exchange included the same processes that I had been planning earlier for my students.

## Collect

My husband, Charlie, started "collecting" long before this short episode of inquiry. He has watched birds since he was a child, and has read about them for years. In his early twenties he helped a local bird-bander tally the birds that visited her mist nets. After college he applied to get a bird-bander's license himself. On this particular walk the sighting of the crow became the observation that instigated a process of inquiry.

## Question

After seeing the crow, my husband sensed a contradiction: The crow behaved like an adult crow, but it sounded like a juvenile. He asked a question to help him sort out and focus his observations.

## Plan

Once he had recognized the contradictory information about the bird, my husband organized a strategy to resolve the contradiction: He would observe the bird more closely using the binoculars.

## Do

My husband's close observation with the binoculars might be considered an experiment. Mary Budd Rowe (1973) calls this kind of experiment "fact finding," with my husband as the scientist who narrows the data and then tests his hypothesis of whether the crow was, indeed, a juvenile.

## Share

Once Charlie had carried out his strategy of further observation, he immediately handed me the binoculars. He wanted to discuss his "research" findings with me. If, after my own observation, I had claimed the bird to be an adult, I'm sure our joint inquiry would have continued with further observation or a trip to the library or local nature center.

These processes—*collect, question, plan, do,* and *share*—happen when people think scientifically.

## Collect

In my classroom I emphasize two types of collecting: broad and focused. The first is a sweeping type, where the senses are opened wide and the filters switched off. Before our hike my husband had collected broadly for many years, building his general knowledge about birds. I arrange the school day so my students will have time for this kind of collecting, time to explore, to "just read," to play with the Cuisenaire rods, to watch the fish swim in its tank, and to experiment with all sorts of writing. In addition to these arranged times, children "collect" all the time: as they play outside on the monkey bars, as they stack blocks, as they chat in the hallway, as they listen to a story, and as they watch the wind bend the trees. Some teachers refer to this "collecting" as exploration, and they note its importance in all subject areas. For example, teachers who describe science workshop emphasize the need for children to explore before they plan any ordered investigation:

> This is what we call exploration. We may have a general sort of problem, but no real question, no explanation we're trying to test. It's just a getting-to-know-the-possibilities time, a messing-about time—*a very important time.* This is where data come from. This is when patterns emerge, predictions are made, questions and explanations spring up. . . . For most children investigations grow out of explorations.
> (Reardon, in Saul, et al. 1993)

I also encourage a second type of collecting that is focused and requires close attention. When the children focus their collecting, they notice what stands out against the background of their prior knowledge—which parts stand out from the whole as different, contradictory, or confusing. In the context of my husband's broad collecting experience with birds, he noticed a particular crow. I want to help my students learn to collect in this way—to notice details and specifics—but I don't want to intrude on their broad exploration. It's a fine line. Jeanne Reardon walked this line adeptly when her class was riveted to the windows of their classroom watching raindrops. She said to the class, "Look at the glass; don't look through it" (1993). She showed them how to observe the raindrops; she didn't notice for them.

How do I help the children notice? How do I do so without imposing too much of my own focusing? How do I show them the "window," show them how to collect, and where and how to look?

I teach the children to "collect" as they look at books, read books, and listen to me read aloud.

## Looking at Books

Before we open a book in my classroom, my students and I begin to notice, observe, and collect. We examine the cover of a book, and spend time sharing what each student notices. Children notice the size and shape of the book, the colors on the cover, the details of any cover illustration, the title and author's name, the placement of the title on the cover, anything and everything. I allow a lot of time for this type of noticing, and it's worth every second. As the children share what they notice with one another, they begin to observe more closely. They sharpen each other's collecting skills. The students attach value to close observation because I allocate time, the precious classroom commodity, for it.

As they read, the students transfer this heightened ability. In language arts the ability to notice shows up in letters exchanged between partners who read the same book:

> Peter, did you see on page fourteen—those trees that look like monsters? (Chad)

> Peter, did you notice the illustrator made the snake look big by making the snake out of the picture? (Chad)

## Reading Aloud

As I read aloud to my class, I teach my students how to collect or notice the "word tools" that writers use to convey clear pictures to readers, just as my husband teaches me how to collect the tools of an ornithologist. I note examples of sense detail, comparisons (metaphors and similes), dialogue, repetition, and exaggeration. Charlie collects flight patterns, silhouettes, coloration, and songs. In the classroom we accumulate a list of these word tools. Once the children can recognize these tools, I ask them to raise a hand when they hear examples as I read aloud. Initially, I stop reading so children can share what they noticed. But after a few books, I don't stop when hands rise but merely nod in acknowledgment. Students who didn't hear the example see their classmates' hands and focus their attention. In this way my students' ability to notice is sharpened during read-aloud times and eventually shows up in letters to one other about books:

> On page ten I could see mad, too, when the book said, "The eyes were as black as lightning." (Colin)

> Did you hear the comparison "with a wind that blows like the wind of the sea," on page fifty-eight? (Rachel)

## Asking Questions

Questioning is central to the process of "doing" science. After my husband focused on the crow during our hike, he asked a question that guided his subsequent "finding out."

> Science discovery is driven by questions. What we do is a response to the questions we are considering.
> (Pearce, in Saul, et al. 1993)

People who write about teaching or learning note the importance of questions. But for a long time educational research focused on teachers' questions. Teachers ask questions to make their students think and to evaluate what students know. Only recently have we examined the questions that *students* ask. Researchers who study the way children learn science note that "questioning is the most important part of science education" (Flatow, in Saul and Jagusch 1992). After many years of expecting children to learn science with questions from a book or teacher, teachers and researchers now realize that students' "inquiries should start with questions or hypotheses that are clear to the children and are posed by them" (Scott 1993). "They should develop confidence that they can ask questions and can find things out for themselves" (Rutherford 1992).

## Asking Questions to Link Science and Reading

The children in my class ask similar questions as they do science and when they read. Their science questions stem from the fundamental questions: *What does the world mean?* and *How does the world work?* (Wellman, in Costa 1991) writes that "science is the process of making meaning." Similarly, children's questions as they read center on *What do these words mean? What do these words tell me about the world?* Regie Routman (1988) writes that "reading for meaning should underlie all encounters with print." Both science and reading processes help children make meaning of the world, so these processes can directly support one another.

Examples from my classroom and field trips illustrate this interconnection and mutual support. For instance, if my students observe live grasshoppers extensively before we read about grasshoppers, their reading experience changes markedly. They may find contradictions between what they observe and what they read. Controversies arise and they ask questions: "Can grasshoppers really stand on two legs? What happens to them in the winter? What do they eat? What happens when they get hungry? How much do they eat?" The children's scientific observations provide a genuine purpose for reading. If the reader then returns to observe the live insects, the scientific observations become more focused. When a child visits the aquarium to observe the animal she is researching, she observes more purposefully. She watches closely and counts how often the dolphin breathes if she has read conflicting information about the frequency. Another child carefully counts the toes on a salamander's back legs because he hasn't been able to find that information in a book. New questions may arise as the children seek to answer their questions at the zoo or aquarium which, in turn, may send them back to a book.

When the children observe closely—scientifically—it not only increases the amount of knowledge they bring to reading, it helps them organize the new information they encounter as they read. Questions that they form from their observations not only create a purpose for reading, they help the children focus and organize a specific strategy for their reading. Likewise, reading helps the children focus and organize strategies for scientific investigation.

## Asking Questions for Whole-Class Discussions

Questions can turn discussions into investigations. The children in my classroom ask the questions that initiate and guide our discussions. My role is to model the constant search for inconsistencies, contradictions, and confusions of our classroom life together. At first I supply a question that begins a discussion, but before long, the students want to discuss their own questions. These questions may stem from science observations in our room, books that students are reading, or situations at home:

Why are the feces of the class fish orange?
How can we stop the gullies from forming on the playground?
Is R.L. Stine a good writer?
Are horror stories okay for children to read?
Should parents tell their children what to watch on television?
Should children have to wear safety helmets when they ride bicycles?

When children ask the questions that guide discussions, they invest their attention and energy into finding out the answers.

## Do: Predict

Prediction is a vital part of the scientific process. Before my husband looked at the crow through binoculars, he predicted that upon closer observation, the crow would have the coloration of either a juvenile or an adult. Predictions guide scientific investigation. Charlie's prediction determined exactly how he would look at the bird. Proficient readers ask: What do I think will happen next? Readers' predictions determine how they will read. Predictions establish the children's purposes for reading, and the act of reading becomes a scientific investigation.

The children in my classroom share predictions about what they read in letters to their reading partners:

> I think Sarah will stay because she had made all those promises. (Chad)

> I think she [Sarah] is going to come back. Do you? I do. (Greg)

## Do: Discuss

Discussions can be another strategy for finding out answers to questions and for determining whether predictions are accurate. Talking can become part of an investigation. During our crow hike Charlie told me of his confusion about the crow as soon as he noticed the contradiction. Jenny Feely (in Scott 1993) describes the role of talk in science:

> The importance of talk in the science session cannot be overstated. Talking about the investigation is crucial to clarifying thoughts. . . . In explaining their ideas they gain a sense of mastery over the ideas they are discussing. Talking also

enables questions to be raised. Considering these questions leads to further investigation—and the process rolls on.

During these discussions the children learn that it's important to notice confusion and contradiction in stories and in the life of the classroom. They also learn that their questions are important enough for the group to discuss and that talking with peers can help answer questions. These lessons about the importance of discussions parallel Wahlqvist's observations as a medical scientist:

> . . . in science, it is increasingly impossible to do work alone. . . . [Besides] needing a team around one to do work, it is very important . . . that debate, discussion, review of primary data can be taking place all the time.
>
> (in Williams 1989)

After many discussions this year, my students talked about what makes a good discussion. Their comments show they understand the importance of controversy and contradiction to a worthwhile discussion:

> [A good discussion] is something that people have nos about and say yes about. There's no discussion if everyone agrees. (Zak)

> [A good discussion] is when you're confused about something that you don't quite understand. You might want to bring that as a discussion question because it might be hard for you. (Clay)

Bruce Wellman (in Costa 1991) also believes that controversy makes discussions worthwhile:

> Conflicting ideas, explanations, and theories often emerge during such sessions. . . . Conflicting theories become fodder for thought and discussion. It is here that teachers explore why students think as they do, and help students to articulate the reasons behind their conclusions.

Science is a social activity in which talk, conflict, controversy, and contradiction play important roles. The children in my class realize that discussions are a strategy for investigating contradictions, answering questions, and clarifying confusions.

## Do: Write

The children in my class also write to investigate, often in letters they write to one another. Sometimes they share with their pen pals a hypothesis about the story. In other letters they explore a confusion that they have not figured out yet, and they look to their pen pals for ideas:

Why doesn't the papa sing anymore? (Chad)

Papa does not sing anymore because he forgets. (Peter)

Why didn't she draw a picture of herself sliding down the dune? (Abby)

Maybe the reason she didn't draw a picture of herself is because she misses her brother and she's thinking about him. (Rachel)

## Share

Scientists share their discoveries with one another. Once my husband had looked through the binoculars at the crow, he shared his findings with me. In the same way, children in my class share their conclusions about reading with one another. During a discussion about Chapter Five in Ann Cameron's book *The Stories Julian Tells*, members of a small group chose to discuss the rising tension of the story that the class describes as a "problem bump" and whether or not Cameron left readers in suspense at the end of the chapter. One child, Abby, shares what she has collected about the story. She has already formulated a question, predicted the answer, and tested it by reading. She is now ready to *share* it. Abby begins: "The end of the chapter could have been a cliffhanger. I need to draw a picture. (She gets a small chalkboard, chalk, and eraser from a bin.) . . . It could've been just like that."

FIGURE 5–1

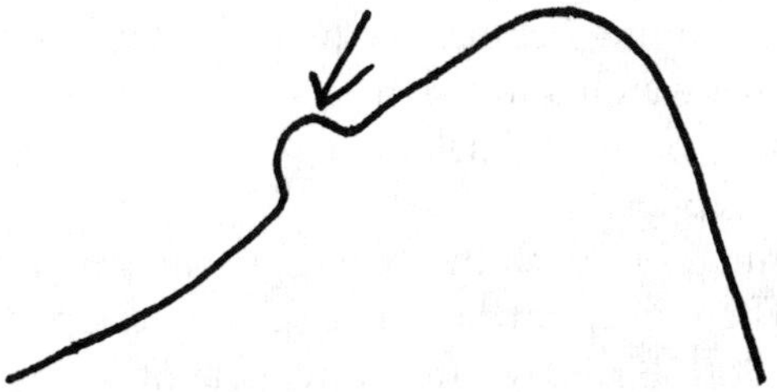

**FIGURE 5–2**

> It could have been a cliffhanger or it could have been like this. It could have been a little problem bump and then go up again. It could have been a cliffhanger or just a little bump.

Physicists Bohm and Peat (1987) note the importance of sharing to research:

> Scientists are actively engaged in their daily work with a social exchange of ideas and opinions through discussions, lectures, conferences, and published papers.

Because I think that collaboration is also integral to reading, I arrange time for my students to read with a partner. In this way they learn the fun of having someone nearby ready to laugh at an illustration, discuss a confusing part, or help sound out a word. As the children research animals in the spring, they share discoveries—"Your animal eats my animal!"—with desk mates. In my classroom the children share at all stages of the science and reading processes: as they collect, sort and focus, plan, and carry out investigations.

## Looking Back

A year has passed since the crow hike. And again my husband and I are investigating the natural world. Only now I wonder how my role as both investigator and teacher affects the way I help my students find out about the world.

Early one recent morning Charlie silently points to the shutter outside the bedroom window. At first I cannot tell what he sees. Then I notice the tip of a pointed, feathered tail—the tail of one of the mourning doves that has been calling at daybreak for the past week. The tail flicks back and forth, and a deep cooing begins. We hear the shutter rattle as another dove joins the first. We watch and listen.

"What are they doing?" I ask.

"Watch," he replies.

I keep watching, but with the curtain in the way I can see only one tail. More cooing. Then more rattling. I see two overlapped tails jiggle for a moment and then both birds fly off in a whistle of wings.

"Were they mating?" I ask.

Charlie nods and gives a short explanation of bird reproduction—cloacae, oviducts, egg formation. Before he finishes explaining, my mind wanders back to last summer when mourning doves nested on our back porch. A year ago we watched two doves carry grass from the neighbors' yards and place it in a hanging planter. As we watched the doves, they were wary and poised to fly. But before long the doves grew used to the back door swinging toward the plant, and they no longer flew off. Instead they watched us with shiny, black eyes.

"How long will it take before they lay eggs?" I wondered. Charlie was not around to answer my question, so I searched for a familiar field guide on the bookshelf. I found Doves–Mourning in the index and turned to the right page, but the answer was not there.

After that I checked the nest each morning, and in several days I noticed two white eggs with a dove sitting dutifully on them. Other questions popped into my mind: How does the mother get food if she's on the nest all the time? Is the male feeding the female? Any time I went into the kitchen during the next week, I watched the nest closely. But I never saw the mate bring her food. How was she doing it? Was she going without food while she sat on the eggs? Was she leaving them to get food at night when it was cold? That didn't make sense.

Then one evening as I waited for dinner to cook, I stood in the doorway watching the nest. I saw one dove fly in and watched the one that had been on the nest fly off. "Charlie! Come here and see this! What's going on?"

He shrugged and mentioned another field guide on our shelf—this time one about birds' nests. I ran to the bookshelf, and sure enough, I read: "Incubation by both sexes; 13–14 days. Female normally incubates from dusk to dawn, when male replaces her" (Harrison 1975). So it wasn't the mother I had been concerned about, but the father!

Once the eggs hatched, they became the news I shared with anyone who asked how I was. My seventy-year-old neighbor happened to ask, so I invited her into the kitchen to see the nestlings. I told her all about how I had discovered the shared arrangements of the male and female.

As I think back to this year of mourning dove discoveries, I notice that my own process of discovery paralleled my students'. My questions were real—based on my direct experience and curiosity—and they led not only to answers, but to more questions. I planned the strategy for answering those questions (e.g., ask an expert, look in a book, and observe directly) based on my question. I made predictions. When my husband-teacher wasn't around, I was just as effective at finding answers, perhaps even more so, because I had to depend on my own ability, not on his expertise. When books didn't offer answers, I devised my own strategies for finding answers. Once I had answered some of my questions, I wanted to share the excitement of my discovery with someone other than my husband. After all, he already knows about birds. But above all, I realize that this genuine kind of finding out takes time, lots of time.

I also notice my husband's role as an effective teacher. On that first day of seeing the doves mating, he helped me notice by pointing out the window. But he let me see the birds myself. He did not answer my initial questions directly, but instead he encouraged me to sort and focus myself, to find my own questions and answers. Several times he suggested ways that I might find those answers, but it was up to me to follow through. When he did try to explain the details of bird reproduction, my mind soon focused on my personal experience with mourning doves.

Our behaviors offer powerful lessons about teaching and learning—lessons about letting the learner ask the questions and take the initiative to answer them. These processes of finding out aren't linear, nor entirely predictable. But I think the processes—collecting, sorting and focusing, planning, doing, sharing—are basically the same, no matter what the age of the student. I think that I find out about the world in the same ways as my students, whether we're finding out about birds or books.

My neighbor and I watch the nest intently.

"And how long before they leave the nest?" she asks.

I look at her. "I have no idea. Come over and watch with me, and we'll find out."

## Bibliography

Bohm, D. and F.D. Peat. 1987. *Science, Order and Creativity: A Dramatic New Look at the Creative Roots of Science and Life*. New York: Bantam Books.

Cameron, A. 1981. *The Stories Julian Tells*. New York: Knopf.

Clark, C.E. and B.J. Sternberg. 1980. *Math In Stride*, Book Two. Menlo Park, CA: Addison-Wesley.

Feely, J. 1993. "Writing in Science." In *Science & Language Links: Classroom Implications*, ed. J. Scott. Portsmouth, NH: Heinemann.

Flatow, I. 1992. "Reflections on Science, Children, and Books." In *Vital Connections: Children, Science, and Books*, ed. W. Saul and S.A. Jagusch. Portsmouth, NH: Heinemann.

Harrison, H. 1975. *A Field Guide to Birds' Nests*. Boston: Houghton Mifflin.

Hyde, A.A. and M.M. Bizar. 1989. *Thinking in Context: Teaching Cognitive Processes Across the Elementary School Curriculum*. White Plains, NY: Longman.

Padilla, M., K.D. Muth, and R. Padilla. 1991. "Science and Reading: Many Process Skills in Common?" In *Science Learning: Process and Applications*, ed. C.M. Santa and D. Alvermann. Newark, DE: International Reading Association.

Pearce, C. 1993. "What If. . . ?" In *Science Workshop: A Whole Language Approach*, ed. W. Saul et al. Portsmouth, NH: Heinemann.

Reardon, J. 1993. "Developing a Community of Scientists." In *Science Workshop: A Whole Language Approach*, ed. W. Saul et al. Portsmouth, NH: Heinemann.

Routman, R. 1988. *Transitions: From Literature to Literacy*. Portsmouth, NH: Heinemann.

Rowe, M.B. 1973. *Teaching Science as Continuous Inquiry*. New York: McGraw-Hill.

Rutherford, F.J. 1992. "Vital Connections: Children, Science, and Books." In *Vital Connections: Children, Science, and Books*, ed. W. Saul and S.A. Jagusch. Portsmouth, NH: Heinemann.

Saul, W. and S.A. Jagusch, eds. 1992. *Vital Connections: Children, Science, and Books*. Portsmouth, NH: Heinemann.

Saul, W., J. Reardon, A. Schmidt, C. Pearce, D. Blackwood, and M.D. Bird. 1993. *Science Workshop: A Whole Language Approach*. Portsmouth, NH: Heinemann.

Scott, J., ed. 1993. *Science & Language Links: Classroom Implications*. Portsmouth, NH: Heinemann.

Stewart-Dore, N. 1993. "Ways of Reading Science." In *Science & Language Links: Classroom Implications*, ed. J. Scott. Portsmouth, NH: Heinemann.

Wahlqvist, M. 1989. "Scandals and Winds of Change." In *The Uncertainty Principle: Australian Scientists Talk about Their World and Our Future*, ed. R. Williams. Sydney: Australian Broadcasting Corporation.

Wellman, B. 1991. "Making Science Learning More Science-Like." In *Developing Minds, Vol. 1: A Resource Book for Teaching Thinking*, introduction by A.L. Costa. Alexandria, VA: Association for Supervision and Curriculum Development.

# 6 Barbara Caplan

# Connections

I love teaching; it is my life. Although in my earliest years of teaching I found comfort and security in the standard curriculum, as my skills and confidence grew I began to sense that there was something more. The enthusiasm I felt as I anticipated each new year, pulling out familiar materials and creating new ones, meeting new students and taking pride in fond remembrances of their siblings, gave me an awareness of the possibility of connecting former learning experiences with current tasks, thereby laying the groundwork for future learning experiences.

I had seen little, if any, change in the science curricula for the first eighteen years I taught in Baltimore County, Maryland. In my fifth-grade classroom, we studied physical and chemical changes; ecosystems; body systems; your changing self; energy; and the use and abuse of non-food substances. Though comprehensive and partially hands-on, these units were clearly outdated, and I spent many happy hours supplementing them. But they also seemed compartmentalized, separated into strict, unrelated categories, and that began to bother me.

I thought of my science teaching in terms of a series of bulletin boards. In September, I would tack up an elaborate display of ecosystems pictures and concepts. This would come down in November, to be replaced by an arrangement of chemistry-related materials. Beakers would be substituted for seines, litmus paper would replace field guides. I had a crazy idea that with this approach, students wouldn't be distracted by any thought of the previous unit and "room" would be made for "new" information.

Then came the whole-language approach that challenged my teaching philosophy and methods. Teachers were encouraged to incorporate the language skills of the tried-and-true curriculum guide with a literature-based approach to reading. After years of teaching the same units and readers, this new take on learning sounded exciting and enervating! A wonderful transformation began, first in my thinking and perceptions about teaching, then in my classroom structure, and finally in my students' responses and involvement.

Literature-based study transferred easily to our science curriculum as novels were related to science. *Island of the Blue Dolphins* by Scott O'Dell, Elizabeth George Speare's *Sign of the Beaver*, and *Hatchet* by Gary Paulsen were rich with details of the natural world and filled with scientific and ecological challenges and questions. The connections seemed natural and right.

At this time homogenous classes were discontinued and I had further impetus to change. Now, instead of thirty fifth-graders reading on the same grade level, I found myself teaching a combination of learning disabled, average, and gifted children.

As I listened to the mirage of courses my cohorts were pursuing in preparation for new teaching approaches, I began wondering where my interests should develop. Then I received a brochure from my student teacher announcing the Elementary Science Integration Project at the University of Maryland Baltimore County. During the first summer of the project, July 1991, my thoughts turned not only toward the integration of language and reading with science, but to an intermingling of science units across the school year. Could this idea of connecting concepts increase my students' understanding of science content?

Somehow, the question tapped into where the excitement of learning dwelled within me. There was something about the year after year experience of building upon knowledge and method and of looking for answers to puzzles remaining in June that enriched the classroom experience the following year. I knew this feeling, anticipated and welcomed it each year. The desire to make connections found voice and focus, and I decided to realign my teaching. The idea of helping children to become more responsible learners, taking control of their questions, played in my mind. How to establish an ownership of discovery became my goal. It occurred to me that when we teach other disciplines, such as mathematics or language, we constantly depend on past knowledge to help our students grasp new ideas. But with my "bulletin board" approach, I was inadvertently suggesting to students that science was compartmentalized; each unit was independent and unrelated to the others. Never did the children seem to connect previous information to what they were learning at the time. Or maybe they were, and I was missing it.

At ESIP, people began posing questions about my questions. Our mission was to plan, develop, and present workshops and articles that would promote the teaching practices integral to inquiry-based science, curriculum integration, and student-centered classrooms. My personal mission was to accept the fact that I no longer had to know all the answers to my students' questions. In fact, I had to become comfortable with the idea that self-discovery and student-generated questions and research were meaningful teaching tools. In our discussion groups, we were encouraged to list every possible question, and no one in the group was permitted to give advice or information. How difficult this was for a teacher who was trained to solve every problem known to man and small children!

I posed my "project question": How can I motivate children to use previous knowledge from science units to increase their discovery and learning in other units? Now the challenge became how to motivate the students to realize that all science can be related. In the actual world of science, our most important claims come from the building upon knowledge, often from one field to another. Experts devise methods to teach mathematics to biologists and biology to chemists. So the integration of knowledge in the classroom seemed like a natural and important process to stress.

In true ESIP style, I began to list my personal queries about my central question. How could I present this quandary so that my students would want to participate? Would it matter in which order I presented the units? Would a particular unit tie better to another if taught in a certain order? How should these discoveries be recorded? Would our tried and true journal approach be useful, or should I rely on verbal feedback? Would I be able to use the information gathered the preceding year in my instruction for this year? Should I share my own connections or simply rely on the children's discoveries? Would all of our fifth-grade units have natural connections, or would some be totally independent of others? As I deliberated over this seemingly insurmountable task, I continued to shuffle displays of bulletin board materials, science equipment, and teaching activities from one unit to the next.

The breakthrough came as we began a lesson on density of liquids. We took a class vote on which liquid would float, oil or water. Five children voted that the oil would be lighter than the water, while twenty-six said that because of the heavy consistency of the oil, it would surely sink. In groups they were to experiment with their fluids to discover what they could about the problem. Casually I asked the five who voted for oil to discuss and elaborate on their thinking. Eureka! Their conclusion had come from their study of water pollution. "The motor oil we poured on the water just laid on top," Nick said, "so I thought that the cooking oil would do the same."

I was delighted with Nick's connection. The longer I teach, the more excited and respectful I become of the creativity and resourcefulness of children. How often do they have the skills and methods we fervently search for? It was then that I decided to let my class in on my research idea. After all, wasn't this classroom a partnership? How often had I marveled at the fact that I learned as much, if not more, from my students as they learned from me? Didn't I often find myself saying, "I didn't know that. Tell me more." If I wanted my children to feel like scientists, shouldn't they be privy to my research and discoveries?

I was so excited by this density-pollution connection that I immediately shared with these budding scientists my research dilemma. "How can we use previous knowledge to increase our comprehension of scientific concepts?" When told that this research would be shared with other teachers, the children decided to extend their journal keeping as a way of helping to document our progress.

Although I had listened to other teachers discuss various uses of scientific journals, I had never used them for purposes other than language or reading. In the past, my students had kept daily journals to record feelings, reactions, and secrets, all nongraded by their teachers. As a class we discussed the issue; students decided that they would make a separate booklet called "Scientific Response Log" with the question on the cover, "What connections do I make while studying fifth-grade science?" They would date their entries and record each time they drew on previous knowledge to arrive at a conclusion or related thought. They could write a sentence, a paragraph, or draw a picture. No entry would be judged or graded, and they could hand the journal in to me at any time, although I would collect all booklets at the conclusion of our last unit.

Being a heterogeneous group of gifted, average, and learning disabled youngsters, the responses were wide and varied. Some students seemed to feel competitive about writing more entries than others at their table. A few less graphically inclined children decided to keep an audiotape of their responses. Some handed in just one or two responses by year's end, and others had "misplaced" their journals and had to have them replaced. But I found the results encouraging.

> 1/10/94   Today we tied in filter paper to Chemistry and Ecosystems. We talked about mixtures in chemistry and we put a mixture in a cup and tried to separate it. And in Ecosystems, a guy came and took some water from lakes and rain water and cleaned it by taking the dirt and bugs from it.

> 1/14/94   In Body Systems we learned your stomach is made of acids. In Chemistry we talked about acids.

> January 10, 1992   Last week, we were talking about how oil stays on top of water in an experiment to see if oil was lighter than water. This connects Ecosystems and Chemistry, because oil spills have to do with the environment, and the experiment was Chemistry.

> January 14, 1992   Today we tested water with litmus paper to see if it was acid or base. Litmus paper can be used to test water; which connects Ecosystems and Chemistry.

> February 28, 1992   If your face is in the sun too much, it loses its elasticity. Today we did an experiment with saliva, corn starch, and water. We did experiments in Chemistry and this is Body Systems. A few days ago, we ate malt balls to experiment with digestion, and it melted in our mouths which is a physical change.

Often a particular lesson would stimulate class discussion of a connection, and after this, I would see children writing their interpretation of the class conversation. When we discussed the role of ptyalin in the saliva for breaking down starches to sugar during digestion, a child quickly looked up his definition of "enzyme" in his chemistry vocabulary, and asked if ptyalin earned the label of enzyme beacuse it precipitated a chemical change.

The children were particularly impressed with the vast variety of chemicals and acids the liver, stomach, and intestines emit during digestion. They decided to pursue an investigation into the effects of our laboratory enzymes on the compost heap we had started in October. Their research began with a question: Will enzymes speed up the decomposition of biodegradable trash? They quickly learned the importance of a control sample and of allowing enough time to carry out their experiment. Sure enough, the students began to see the process of decay accelerated by the costly chemicals. This important observation led to questions about whether a process can be considered commercially viable.

> June 1, 1993   We tried our chemistry chemicals on our compost heap. Boy does that thing disgust me! The chemicals speed the decomposition a lot but Jake said it cost too much money and I think he's right.

Discovering our dependence on the ecosystem for our health and welfare provided an appreciation for the environment. Comparing the harmful effects of drug abuse on our bodies with the harmful effects of pollution on the food chain increased an understanding of the misuse of chemicals. During the study of energy sources, many children saw the necessity of tapping our material resources as alternatives to expendable sources. Often I found it helpful to pose a question in order to stimulate reflection on certain topics. Teacher-directed webs and graphic organizers also facilitated responses.

Previously, our writer's workshop was spent writing fanciful or factual stories about what might, could, and did happen to ten-year-olds. I allowed free thought and choice during the three periods per week we undertook this activity. Sometime during the middle of the year, stories of scientific discoveries, inventions, and wonderings began to appear. Although the majority of these were fantasy, I noticed many scientific facts creeping into students' accounts. These children were applying science quite naturally in their creative writing!

> Have you ever thought about bugs? I know what you're thinking—yuck! But that's not true! They kill a lot of bad things for us. They are important! Think about it—no bugs. Sounds pretty good, huh? Not necessarily. You probably have pets, right? Well, lots of pets and food (such as fish and crabs), eat bugs to survive.

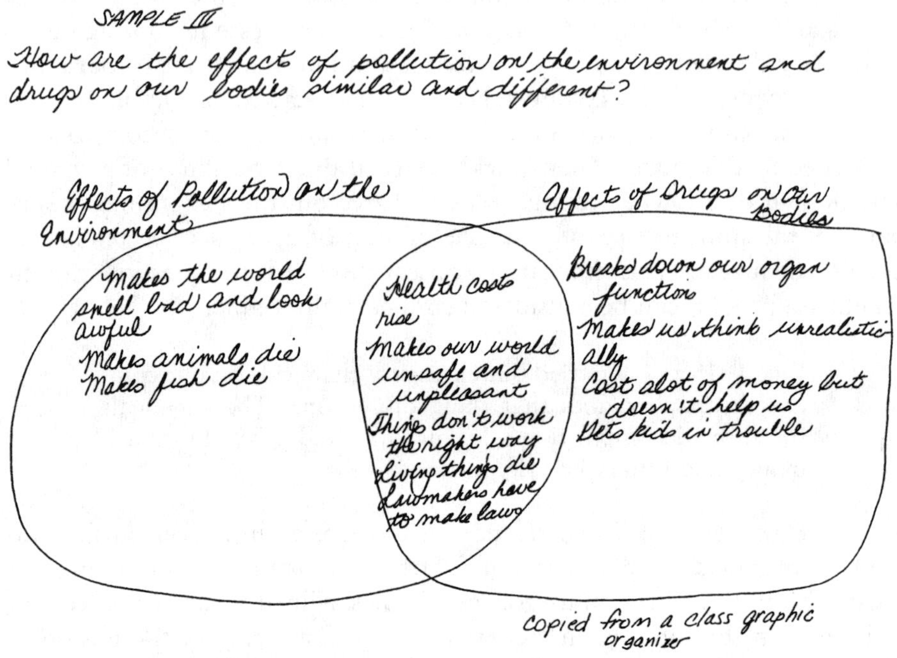

SAMPLE III

How are the effects of pollution on the environment and drugs on our bodies similar and different?

Effects of Pollution on the Environment

- Makes the world smell bad and look awful
- Makes animals die
- Makes fish die

Health costs rise

Makes our world unsafe and unpleasant

Things don't work the right way

Living things die

Lawmakers have to make laws

Effects of Drugs on our bodies

- Breaks down our organ function
- Makes us think unrealistically
- Cost alot of money but doesn't help us
- Gets kids in trouble

copied from a class graphic organizer

FIGURE 6–1

So, next time a spider crawls on you, don't scream and flick it off! Thank it! Think about it!

Debra Bunn (see Chapter 4) gave me the idea of approaching science in a playful manner by having us dissect squid, purely to discover whatever we could find in this easily attainable marine animal. Deciding to expand on her wonderfully creative idea, I secured thirty books from the library about marine life. After distributing the books, the children set out to explore how trade books work by using the cover, table of contents, and index. Since we had just finished reading *Island of the Blue Dolphins*, students had many wonderings about marine animals mentioned in the story. During this browsing/investigation, one group of four children decided to design an ecosystem for the octopus. Another group wanted to cross-reference, to discover how various pollutants might affect specific marine populations. Writer's workshop stories about underwater life proliferated!

### Dissecting a Squid

*Chris Borcik, June 6, 1994*

"Today we will be dissecting a squid," announced Ms. Caplan.

Her class had been waiting for this day (except for Allison). "Please get a tray, scissors, and a pencil," she continued. "Read your paper and begin. Remember scientists don't say oooh, they say aaah."

"Cool," yelled Andy from across the room. "I think mine's still alive!"

"Gross me out!" said Allison disgustedly.

When they cut their squid open they saw almost all the organs and body parts in the squid.

"The squid's beak and mouth are under its tentacles," explained Ms. Caplan. "Try to find these parts of the squid: eyelids, ink pouch, liver, and a pen with which you can write. When you find these you can write whatever you want with the pen and search through the squid. If you have any questions, ask the person next to you or myself."

"Where is the pen?" asked Chad.

"You'll have to find that out for yourself," said Ms. Caplan.

The first person to find everything was Jake. He had two pens in his squid instead of one.

"That wasn't so bad," sighed the relieved Allison.

"Next week, we'll be dissecting Jeff," exclaimed Ms. Caplan. "Just kidding, Jeff."

When we actually dissected the squid, I provided the students with a diagram and instruction sheet to guide their operation. A number of children commented that the digestive tract had some similarities with the chart in their math teacher's room. (She was in the process of teaching the fifth-grade body systems unit.) The students' observation left me again thinking about tying the squid dissection to our body systems unit. No sooner had I thought it than a small group of children approached me with the very same idea. Talk about a child-centered classroom! In my early days of teaching, I remember thinking, "How will I ever come up with enough ideas to keep an entire class of students happily occupied and challenged for an entire year?" Years of experience have helped me turn some of that responsibility over to creative young minds. If we, as teachers, took time to listen to what children want to learn, curriculum would be written easily and compellingly!

As the year progressed, the students often asked if they could note connections from our novels, assemblies, videos, and various speakers in their journals. When we read *Sign of the Beaver* and *Hatchet*, the children noted how the main characters came to depend on the ecosystems of their areas for their survival. Our graphic organizer compared and contrasted the similarities and differences of the ecosystems.

When I invited speakers, I asked them to consider our previous units of study in their presentation. They seemed to appreciate the knowledge of the students and were quick to draw connections in their delivery. A young man from the National Geologic Survey, for instance, discussed the chemical composition of our rivers, oceans, and lakes, as well as the impact of pH on plant and animal life. An expert on whales brought marine skeletons and compared the bones to our own body structure and chemical composition.

> April 18, 1991    Today, Mrs. Harcourt came and talked to us about whales. Even though it does not seem like it would connect to any science units, it did, and these are some of them: 1) Whales live in a water ecosystem, and we studied ecosystems. 2) We talked about the whale's digestive, circulatory, and respiratory systems. 3) We compared things in chemistry and body systems. 4) We talked about blubber being fat and we talked about fat in body systems.
>
> I thought it was interesting when we talked about how whales could have once been land mammals. Now I know a lot more about whales. I am glad Mrs. Harcourt came.

During the question and answer session following a dentist's lecture, several students politely asked when and how he would connect his subject to other science information we had studied. He never did, and they judged this lecture not as successful as some of the others.

Students' journals took different forms, sometimes serving as cues or notes. Shelley's journal was a hodge-podge of one-sentence statements. "We tested nutrient water from intestines." "Molecules are in chemistry, environment, and bodies." "Drugs are chemicals." Her written statements did little to explain her understanding of concepts, but when asked to explain verbally, she comfortably elaborated on the connections she made.

Taking this important cue from Shelley, I wondered if a chart of simple, child-generated statements should be compiled throughout the year and displayed daily.

The journals were not the only means of record keeping. Each Friday, my students wrote letters to me that I answered and returned on Monday. Often, the text of their letters included observations, questions, and feelings about our science studies.

> April 2, 1993
> Dear Ms. Caplan,
>     I been thinking a lot about the ecosystems. I would like to take a field trip to the following:
>     a tundra
>     Brian Hatchet
>     Karana's island dolphin
>     where the tribes live
> I know we can't but just in case, can we?
>
>                                        Love,
>                                        Tanya
>     P.S. write back

When we embarked on a study of molecules during our unit on physical and chemical changes, Elissa commented that when she learned about molecules in third grade, they made no sense. Now, she suddenly understood the concept. As educators, we assume that children are developmentally ready for what our curriculum presents. But initial exposure often turns to mastery at a later age.

With this idea in mind, could learning possibly be further investigated and enhanced by providing "boxes" of the previous grades' science equipment? I often had the feeling that my fifth graders were not finished with mystery powders when I chose to put them away. If the paraphernalia were available, would the learning be extended and new discoveries be made independently? Isn't this how scientists work?

Connecting concepts and knowledge became a natural, easy way for children to raise their own questions and seek meaningful answers. Learning became contagious, sparks of interest bounced around the classroom. At the end of the year, when asked to write letters to incoming fifth graders, one child wrote, "In Mrs. Caplan's class, all of the science units are related. If you understand the first one, you've got it made."

Now my "bulletin board" begins in September, wraps around the room, grows more detailed throughout the year, and is always punctuated with a big sign: "To Be Continued."

## Bibliography

Allison, L. 1976. *Blood and Guts: A Working Guide to Your Own Insides.* Boston, MA: Yola Berry Press.

Center for Environmental Education. 1985. *The Ocean . . . Consider the Connections.* Washington, DC: Center for Environmental Education.

Coulombe, D.A. 1984. *The Seaside Naturalist: A Guide to Nature Study at the Seashore.* Old Tappen, NJ: Prentice-Hall.

Fine, J.C. 1987. *Oceans in Peril.* New York: Atheneum.

George, J.C. 1990. *One Day in the Tropical Rain Forest.* New York: Crowell.

Kohl, J. and H. Kohl. 1977. *The View from the Oak.* Boston, MA: Little, Brown and Company.

Madrago, G.M. 1990. *Oceanography for Landlocked Classrooms.* Alexandria, VA: National Association of Biology Teachers.

O'Dell, S. 1978. *Island of the Blue Dolphins.* New York: Dell.

Paulsen, G. 1988. *Hatchet.* New York: Puffin.

Showers, P. 1989. *A Drop of Blood.* New York: Harper and Row.

Speare, E.G. 1993. *Sign of the Beaver.* New York: Dell.

Spurgeon, R. 1988. *Usborne Science and Experiments—Ecology.* Madrid, Spain: Usborne Publishing.

Whale Research Group. 1984. *Getting Along.* Labrador City, Newfoundland: The Whale Research Group.

# 7 Stephanie Terry

# Working in Community

The children in the first-grade class who cocreated our community of readers, writers, and thinkers are all African American. Most have had prekindergarten and kindergarten "school" experience. Their kindergarten lessons, like those in many large urban schools, follow a basal reader approach with a strong emphasis on learning the "prescribed" vocabulary word list and mastering the reading context in the accompanying books. They have done little, if any, writing on their own, except for workbook fill-in-the-blanks and ditto sheets. The average class size for kindergarten was twenty-five to thirty students. While the average first-grade class last year had thirty students, mine had thirty-three. This year twenty-one students are enrolled in my class.

Our school sits overtop a supermarket owned by one of the nation's top African American entrepreneurs. We are part of a small cluster of buildings surrounded by the Madison Square Professional Complex. There are two small convenience stores that sell snacks, sodas, cigarettes, and fast foods, a Korean-owned laundry, a day care center, a beauty parlor, and the rental office for the apartments in the complex. In between these buildings there is a small concrete courtyard where, on sunny days, the children from the day care center come out to play. Our students sometimes join them, and also play on the blacktop area to the left of the school itself.

Most students walk to Duke Ellington Primary School #117 in northwest Baltimore with older siblings or relatives. Others arrive by car and a few travel by public bus service. We are one of the city's few remaining primary schools and provide one class of morning and afternoon pre-K classes, two morning and afternoon kindergarten classes, one level IV classroom for students with special needs, and five first grade classes.

Having struggled with the "structured" basal reader approach to teaching reading and language arts (with my own twist) for nine years, I was curious and anxious to stretch my wings. As I reflected on my teaching, I realized I've often been called "different." I wondered if encouraging my students to see the differences in my teaching style would somehow pave the way for even more exciting learning experiences to happen. There were always those few students, the "top," who were going to make it anyway. Was what I noticed in those quiet, "I-will-do-everything-just-as-the-teacher-says" students really learning, or was it just robot-like memorization? Was it possible to step back and allow the natural learning and curiosity of a child to coexist in a community of learners and thinkers? What would I learn by helping to establish such a community with my students rather than allowing myself or the curriculum guide to be the sole initiator? How would I get parents to support this direction of teaching and extend our classroom to the larger community? How would my own love for teaching, which dwells heavily on Maria Montessori's philosophy for educating the young child, be supported? These were some of the recurring questions I continued to explore.

Armed with individually prepared student journals, a parent/family journal for each child to take home at different times during the school year, loads of high-interest trade books, pictures, magazines, and a video camera, the children and I began the work of building a community of thinkers and learners. The live animals that soon filled our classroom were our partners in this endeavor. Newts, salamanders, fish, tree frogs, a pond frog who developed from a tadpole last year in class, a toad (happily donated by a mom who found it on the wall in her apartment after purchasing a new plant), a large box turtle (he came to visit one day with one of the children and just stayed), a garter snake, and several hermit crabs inhabit our classroom. Cicadas, spiders, a cricket habitat, and mealworms complete our classroom menagerie.

We strengthen the ties to our classroom community each day as we enter the classroom and form our Morning Unity circle. Jwanza Kunjufu (1984) describes a similar circle in his work on developing positive images in young children. The children and I stand quietly, breathing in the excitement of the day's learning and focusing ourselves on the work ahead. We

The Meal Worm Be com a pupd And Then
The Beetl. And Then The Beetle Lay
Eggs And Mrs Treety is Hob
I The kes is Hob to.

**FIGURE 7–1**

greet each other with "Jambo" (Kiswahili) or "Hello," and extend a hand or hug, saying words like, "I'm glad you came today; It's great having you here today; I missed you yesterday, I'm glad you made it today." We then take our seats on the floor, legs crossed, bodies still. We allow ourselves time to get back to our room, our space, our learning. As we sit in the silence of the first moments of the work day, we imagine ourselves working hard, thinking clearly, and doing our best. Slowly we release and let go of the things we don't need, the troubling moments that may have entered our space. When we open our eyes, we are ready to begin.

To help us further establish the "community," we begin our lessons with *Science Talk* (Terry 1991). Each day, the children and I make observations, raise questions, and record our thoughts in journals. When one child wonders aloud about one of our creatures, the other children stretch themselves to get a closer look, and additional questions come pouring from the budding scientists. The children and I move freely between talk, observations, and books to help us know more and ask more. Sometimes I ask a question such as, "What do you think our praying mantis will need to eat?" I asked this question when I brought in a praying mantis I had found on my front lawn. The children's responses included donuts, hot dogs, apples, hamburger, and pork chops. Through our talk, the children were encouraged to think about ways for us to investigate what the praying mantis would eat. The following were among the strategies offered: to ask somebody, ask a scientist, ask a pet store owner, look in a book.

Bianca Lavies' book *Backyard Hunter: The Praying Mantis* inspired us to take a trip to a local pet store to purchase crickets for our praying mantis. The book also provided stimulating real-life photos and text of what the children and I would experience when our praying mantis' ootheca (egg case) hatched. One January morning, the children and I watched as tiny mantids (nymphs) hatched in our classroom. They reminded us of the baby cricket we had observed earlier in the year in our cricket habitat. The excitement mounted as a neighboring class who shared our interest in science giggled with delight as new baby nymphs emerged in their classroom also.

More questions, more observations, more books, and more writing propelled us through the life cycle of the praying mantis as well as that of the mealworms. The thinking and *Science Talk* reflected clear connections between the topics. By the time the Baltimore City Schools' first grade science unit on butterflies arrived in the spring, our classroom "scientists" were truly experts. Since September, they had lived with nymphs, pupas, and metamorphoses.

One of the concepts that threads throughout our room is the gentleness of the children and the "critters." On more than one occasion, when Frank or Jerold have stepped on or pushed a classmate, we shared how our creatures crawl over, walk on, and bump into each other without giving the other a "whack" (most times this is all that we need to refocus our thoughts). Of course, this is not always the case. Our toad reacted vio-

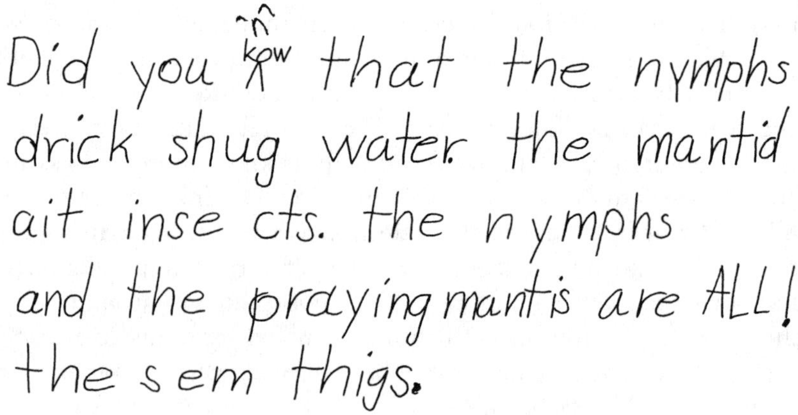

Did you kow that the nymphs
drick shug water the mantid
ait insects. the nymphs
and the praying mantis are ALL!
the sem thigs.

**FIGURE 7–2**

Well how did she lay the eggs
With out the mail?
The nymphs were in a egg case
and the egg case was in
ootheca.
But if she lad the eggs with
out the mail where did
get the spum?
The nymphs where in a egg
case.

FIGURE 7-3

lently to our newly arrived swift (lizard) and the newts have been observed eating a goldfish or two. We discuss these incidents as well, and the children are able to make healthy transitions between classroom learning and real life.

No child is left out of the observation or talk. Any and everyone's answers and thoughts are listened to. Even the shyest in the class edges up to the forefront and hopes to be the one to offer fresh water to the tree frog or feed the toad.

I recall our *Science Talk* one morning in January when the children discovered that the toad had changed colors. All sorts of questions and thoughts arose: "How did that happen? Maybe it's hungry? It didn't eat since Friday. Look, the water in the bowl is gone. I think it's cold, that's why it changed colors." Following this flurry of talk we offered the toad a bowl of fresh water and a few crickets and watched what happened. Within a few minutes, the crickets were gobbled up, and the toad, before our eyes, had miraculously turned from a pale whitish green to its usual greenish brown. Another child commented on how much warmer it had become in our classroom (the heat is lowered over the weekend). I mentioned to the children that the classroom creatures had all been moved to a locked area at the back of the library because the building was being fumigated. The journal entries for that morning were filled with talk about the toad and recommendations as to what we might do the next time the building was to be fumigated.

When the new and larger hermit crabs entered the classroom near the end of September, some of the children who were quite used to the smaller ones, which we had observed shedding their shells and apartment hunting for a roomier model, were a bit apprehensive. These new crabs were almost as large as my fist. Several children prepared the basin with warm water for a "crab bath," others cleaned out the leftover food and placed fresh water and food in the large open aquarium we reserved for the hermit crabs. We had recently read Eric Carle's *A House for Hermit Crab* and several other nonfiction trade books about crabs. The children ooohed and ahhed over the large claw, the cumbersome dragging movement of the new crabs, and the hesitant peeping-out glance they make before daring to venture out. Latisha, who often is found inching her way a few paces behind the circle of children on the floor, noticed and said, "They don't hurt either"; another child piped up, "They always go to Kyle." This prompted everyone to sit like Kyle, one of the shy students. He announced proudly, "That's because I sit still." The children and I learned another lesson: If we want to get along with our new crabs and each other, we must begin to show "heshima" (Kiswahili for respect). The intermittent lessons of Kiswahili began to have even more meaning.

Although some of our classroom creatures may arrive by accident, the children's questions and my quick notes of what happens are sustained by a deliberate selection of books and daily use of journal writing time. Beginning with *The Tree of Life: The World of the African Baobab*, by Barbara Bash, the books are an integral part of our life. Students and parents borrow books from our classroom library to curl up and read together at home where the rhythm of the words and the illustrations can delight both the reader *and* the listener. The *Science Talk* helps to kick off writing, not only in the students' journals but also in my own "big book" journal. I first saw this big book journal last fall in Reston, Virginia when I visited Cherly Chew's first-grade class. This journal is a larger version of the students' with several 24″ × 36″ manila drawing paper sheets that I've stapled together, titled, *My Journal by Mrs. Terry, September 2, 1993*. We write and use the journals to share ideas. As the children watch me struggle to form letters and put ideas together, the hard part of writing and thinking is taking place. The children watch me scratch out, learn to insert carets, and spell-it-like-it-sounds right before their eyes on the page.

I ask and encourage them to help me, as the writer, make my work better. They share ideas on how to make the letters neater, end or begin a thought, add an overlooked detail, and stretch out the sounds of a difficult word. Some students remember the word from our sign language/spelling lessons and others recall seeing the word in the room, on another journal page, or in one of our books. We encourage each other with the notion that it is OK to make a mistake because you can always change your ideas later. The students who were part of my reader response group in September and October helped the class become each other's response group by pairing up with a listener to read, add thoughts, and make changes.

The basal reader, still a required text by our system, goes home as an extra resource. In the classroom library, the children self-select books from informational books about frogs, toads, and snails to *Harriet Tubman*, *Amazing Grace* (a story about a young girl who is encouraged to be anything she likes), and the *Enchanted Hair Tale* (a story of a boy who is made fun of because he wears his hair differently until he meets others like himself).

What makes me most proud of my research is that of this year's twenty-one students, twenty are reading independently from both required books and the variety of material I add to our class. They keep track of their reading with daily reading logs. The parents of my students visit often or call me at home to talk about a lesson. From their very first entries in the parent/family journals, where they expressed their initial concerns and hopes about their children's learning, parents have been involved in our classroom community. Following is the letter I sent to them introducing the journals.

> Dear Parents,
>       Today your child is bringing home for the first time the Parent & Family Journal. As you know, your child writes in a journal here each day at school. From time to time the Parent & Family Journal will come home for you to write in, too. I hope that you will find this experience as exciting as the children do!
>       In class the children pick their own topics about which to write, read to an audience in the Author's Chair, make corrections and additions as they need to, and listen to suggestions to "polish" up their writing. As we do this we *all* get a chance to grow as a community of writers, readers, and thinkers.
>       Please think about the ideas below and write your thoughts in the journal on p. 1 and 2. Then sign your name and the date. Be sure to have your child bring the journal back to school on the next school day. I will read the journals, write back to you, and use it to make our work this year even better!
> * This is a parent/family journal; a parent, grandparent, or adult family member or caregiver may respond.
> Page 1: Now that we have "worked" together for about $2\frac{1}{2}$ months, what would you like for me to *know* about your child that I might not know yet?
> Page 2: What are you most pleased with or most displeased with in regard to our work together with your child?
>       Parent's signature _____ Date _____

*Describe what being a parent of your first grader has been like for the first few weeks of school.*

The first two weeks of school for me and my first grader was kind of rough in the beginning. My daughter was very excited. So excited that she couldn't stop talking at home or in class. It's a new experience for her and me. Because she's at a higher level now, so we have to be on our toes. I have to have a lot of patience when she gets a little confused. Well in all we are both having a good time, because it is different.

### Teacher's Response

Cheri is very excited about school . . . and it's contagious. She's so eager to share and always wants to do her best. It's really a delight to see. I hope that both of you will continue to talk at home about all of the exciting things that Cheri is learning. With your help at home I know that she will continue to have a great year. Please use this journal to help share your thoughts as we move through the year.

Stephanie Terry

They now write about their attitudes for learning and the success of their children.

I'm so glad Charles is a happy child. He has made a big progress with his work and his math is improving very well. When I come home he has his math done.

I am concerned about his spelling. He can't seem to keep in his mind to pronounce his words before and after he spells them. Charles can draw pretty well after I show him on a spare piece of paper and he can do very good.

I do know that Charles tries to rush through his homework, until I tell him to take his time and to write neatly. He enjoys my reading to him and I have noticed he pays attention when I'm reading to him. I'm glad you are his teacher, you are doing very, very well.

### Teacher's Response

Thank you again for *all* of your support. Charles knows that we're both working together to help him to *be* his best. Here in school I shall continue to talk with him about "working fast" vs. "working BEST." He loves reading and math! I'm so glad you two have time to sit together for quiet reading time at home. Charles is getting off to a wonderful start!

Peace,
Stephanie Terry

Happily, the parents' involvement sometimes goes beyond the journals. Another parent, Kelly's mom, came in one day with this announcement: "I had to come in here to see what a newt was. Kel' was trying to explain this to me as a part of her homework last night."

I know that this type of "child-initiated learning" takes more time than the traditional twenty-minute reading groups and skills lessons. I know, too, that as I step back and allow my children to look, listen, and think longer, I learn more about each child. The freedom to move about and make choices about what we learn had not been a primary part of these students' learning. I tell my students that this is the collaborative way college students work. The stern teacher at the front of the room, "all-eyes-ahead" approach placed a lot of pressure on teachers to perform, and on students to react to the performer.

I find I now notice more about my teaching. One strong aspect is the sense of independence that grows from the student. I spend less time on preparing the perfect lesson package and more time on what questions will come from what might happen next. I don't always have to have the right answer. Each child becomes his or her own resource. The books, the people who visit, and the journal writings now drive each child to want to do more. There is also no fluke in the message that learning about ourselves helps us learn more about others.

I would like for each member of our "community" to understand the commitment to learning and passing it on. When Jerold curls up on the floor with Alvin (a somewhat reluctant/moody student), Alvin accepts, questions, and makes the conference time worth his while. When he goes home now, he shares the work with his mom. She, in turn, stops in at least once a week to ask, "Ms. Terry, can you listen to Alvin read this?" I put my pencil down and pull my chair up close to listen as Alvin reads to me, his mom, and his baby sister, after everyone else is gone.

## Bibliography

Adoff, A. 1970. *Malcolm X*. New York: Harper & Row.

Bains, R. 1982. *Harriet Tubman*. Mahwah, NJ: Troll.

Bash, B. 1989. *The Tree of Life: The World of the African Baobab*. Boston: Little, Brown.

Brownell, M.B. 1988. *Busy Beavers*. Washington, DC: National Geographic Society.

Buscaglia, L. 1982. *The Fall of Freddie the Leaf: A Story of Life for All Ages*. Slack. (Distributed by Holt Rhinehart & Co. New York)

Carle, E. 1987. *A House for Hermit Crab*. Saxonville, MA: Picture Book Studio.

DeVeau, A. 1987. *An Enchanted Hair Tale*. New York: Harper & Row.

Elkind, D. 1988. *The Hurried Child—Growing Up Too Fast Too Soon*. Menlo Park, CA: Addison Wesley.

George, J.C. 1991. *The Moon of the Salamander*. New York: HarperCollins.

Greenfield, E. 1988. *Nathaniel Talking*. New York: Black Butterfly Children's Books.

Grifalconi, A. 1987. *Darkness and the Butterfly*. Boston: Little, Brown.

Hoffman, M. 1991. *Amazing Grace*. New York: Dial.

Jordan, T. 1992. *The Journey of the Red-Eyed Tree Frog*. New York: Simon and Schuster.

Kunjufu, J. 1984. *Developing Positive Self-Images and Disciplines in Black Children*, 1st ed. Chicago: African American Images.

Lavies, B. 1989. *Lily Pad Pond*. New York: Dutton.

Lavies, B. 1990. *Backyard Hunter: The Praying Mantis*. New York: Dutton.

Mellonie, B., and R. Ingpen. 1983. *Lifetimes*. New York: Bantam.

Montessori, M. 1964. *The Montessori Method*. New York: Schocken Books.

Price, L. (told by). 1990. *Aida*. San Diego: Harcourt Brace Jovanovich.

Steptoe, J. 1987. *Mufaro's Beautiful Daughters*. New York: William Morrow, Lothrop.

Wright, E. 1989. *Good Morning Class, I Love You*. Torrance, CA: Jalmar Press.

Yoshi. 1987. *Who's Hiding Here?* Saxonville, MA: Picture Book Studio.

# III

# Making It Work

# 8 Donna Dieckman

# How I *Really* Plan

I looked out at the twenty-seven pre-service teachers who seemed to hang on my every word. . . . I was a real teacher, come to share the experiences of real classroom life. Not like the university professor who seemed to float on a cloud of theory above the road they were soon to travel. What could I tell them? I vividly recalled the many 9-step lesson plans I had written as a pre-service teacher. In all truth, they didn't help. I recalled the critical evaluation of curriculum guides— interesting, but removed from the real work of classroom planning. What is it that I DO, they wanted to know.

Planning, for me, begins in the long days of summer. I need to sketch out the big picture before I fill in the details. I try to imagine my class. There are the obvious questions about grade level and number of students. This year, I have thirty first graders. I think back to the previous year and what it felt like to share space with just twenty-five little people. The five additional children assigned to the room this year means that I will need more materials and space for another table. As I imagine little hands grabbing for cotton balls or tongue depressors, I wonder how I will find time to listen to five more students, how to fit in five more conferences each week. That's an important consideration, and one that laces through all my thoughts, all my plans.

Back to the concrete . . . I try to learn what I can about the community from which my students are drawn. Stereotypes serve us poorly in this regard. I recall a summer program for at-risk urban students. Planning was based on the "fact" that the population was predominantly low socioeconomic African American. Plans were made for African studies, tapping into the rich culture of far off lands. With that information I planned to focus on the urban environment, the "concrete forest." Fortunately, I decided to visit the neighborhood before school began. Surprise! The children were predominantly Caucasian and their neighborhood bordered on an extensive inland waterway. All planning was based on the media image of the at-risk urban child and was extremely inappropriate for making meaningful connections to the lives of this particular group of at-risk urban children.

The school where I will teach next year is located in a suburban, relatively affluent area. A closer look reveals that within the community there are also a number of subsidized properties. Who will play with whom is sometimes an issue. This year I will also have two children who speak no English. I need to make sure that from the beginning they have ways to participate in classroom life. There are also the rumors I must heed or ignore—which students are considered terrors, which moms—I have a reputation for not attending too carefully to rumors. Some of my favorite students have been those others have found difficult.

I begin to plan with a map of the room. I have purposely organized areas around the perimeter of the room to maximize floor and work space. This arrangement also helps with traffic flow as children navigate from one area to another. A few areas are strategically placed, such as the science area. Observing six-year-olds trying to carry water across the room for their science investigations convinced me to create our science area in the corner closest to the sink! My current arrangement also lends itself to quick and easy cleanup and restocking of materials.

Our space needs to accommodate the materials we use as well as the pedagogical needs of the children. Though I receive science kits containing basic materials for each unit, it is difficult for children to continue their investigations when the materials must be returned by a certain date. Over the past few years I have made note of materials frequently requested. Now, instead of storage boxes, materials are housed in plastic shoeboxes in our science area. Students can access them without my assistance. The top twenty common materials needed for student investigations include:

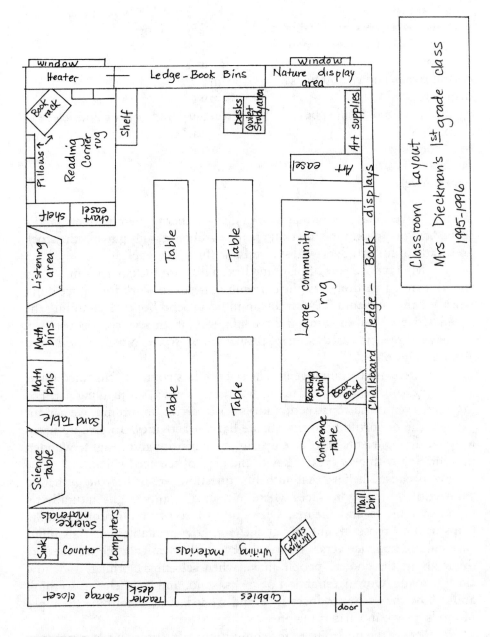

**FIGURE 8–1**

aluminum foil

assorted containers, preferably clear, both large and small

balloons

cotton swabs and cotton balls

dish detergent

eyedroppers and small spoons

flashlights

food coloring

magnets

paper towels

plastic Ziplock™ bags and paper bags

salt and baking soda

sand

seeds

soil

straws

tongue depressors or Popsicle™ sticks

vegetable oil

vinegar

waxed paper

We also have a class set of magnifying glasses, thermometers, rulers, and a scale. Scissors, glue, tape, marking pens, cardboard, and paper—the stock and trade of first graders—must also be within easy reach.

My favorite part of planning has to do with the curriculum. As my friend Jeanne Reardon says, the curriculum needs to work for us, we don't work for the curriculum. With this in mind I spend hours dismantling the mandated program of study and reconfiguring it. In science, for instance, we have three kit-based units: *Constructions*, *Rock, Sand & Soil*, and *Weather and Me*.

There are certain givens. The science kits come at scheduled times and we need to be ready for them, but there is always a juggling act. For instance, even if the construction kit is set to arrive in autumn, we cannot pass up the opportunity to investigate harvest activities. To give up naturally occurring events is to give up natural curiosity and insight. Wonder, that looking with new eyes, is key to the kind of science I value.

Because I believe that authentic questions are born from authentic connections, I look for places where our science units might naturally tie to other subjects and themes. Our study of construction, for example, helps us look more insightfully at shelters, how available materials influence culture and vice versa. As we observe and investigate the weather we think about the choices people make when selecting clothing, and how cloth is made. Our investigation of rocks, sand, and soil helps us to think about how the earth produces food and what factors determine the types of foods grown in various regions.

Seeing the possibilities for connections sometimes leads to a minor dissatisfaction with the mandated curriculum, so I add to it. In the social studies unit on "producers and consumers" I add a strong environmental education component. This addition is actually in keeping with state and national mandates. In truth, I have come to frame our whole year around our scientific studies. We utilize our reading, writing, and math skills to gather information, observe, record, conduct research, and communicate our findings.

I can also benefit from my students' evaluations and insights. Last year my students were not pleased with the weather study. The kit arrived in the winter, when going outside was difficult. It wasn't a good time to lie flat on our backs and observe the clouds. The wonderful dew on fall leaves had passed. In short, the children convinced me that it would be more meaningful and relevant to study the changes in weather throughout the year. We'll still utilize the kit during the winter, when it arrives, to study snow, ice, and freezing water, but we will also make time this year to study weather changes and phenomena as they naturally occur.

Few things make me happier than finding authentic connections. Not only do they make for important and frequently overlooked learning opportunities, but they also enable me to eke out more time for student reflection and conversation. I happily realize that the unit on construction (officially slated to arrive in September) can be tied to the unit on rocks, sand, and soil (a kit to be delivered in March). We can compare and contrast the ways in which humans build and nature builds. Our weather and environmental studies will provide further insight: How does weather affect natural and man-made construction? How do buildings affect the environment?

With the curriculum sketched out I begin to gather resources that support the topics at hand. Often it is a children's book that helps me to think about connections in our curriculum. A few years back I stumbled upon *Talking Walls* by Margy B. Knight. As readers we journey around the world to catch a glimpse of the many walls; it's all there—culture, history, rocks, sand and soil, construction. We share this book during December as a way of celebrating diversity, a pleasant change from the usual holiday fanfare.

Books provide many windows for the children. While investigating construction our class library overflows with books from a wide variety of genres. Side by side are favorite folktales such as *The Three Little Pigs* and *The Three Billy Goats Gruff* and informational favorites such as *How a House Is Built* by Gail Gibbons and *Bridges* by Ken Robbins. Our collection includes historical fiction, poetry, modern classics, experiment books, visual dictionaries, and biographies, as well as folktales and informational texts.

In addition to books I think about human resources and field trips. For instance, for our unit on construction, could I find a plumber to visit the class? Is there a hardware store in the neighborhood that might enjoy a visit? Again, I search for connections: Last year we found a construction in progress. We visited the site where a replica of a slave ship was being built.

My thoughts returned to the pre-service students. If they could learn about their community, plan their rooms and re-sources, and reconfigure their curriculum, would they be able to teach? Would this give them what they need? No, I real-ized. All of the above are the bricks we use to build a struc-ture, but the mortar is in the practices that are set up, the routines that enable the children to move from hour to hour, from day to day. If I had to invent these routines again and again for every lesson, teaching would be impossible.

All of this work, the messing with curriculum, the setting up of the room, the gathering of materials, is what a teacher can plan. But the most important part of what goes on in a classroom has to do with how we, as a community, use those bricks and mortar that I, the teacher, have brought with me. And that, to some extent, cannot be planned.

The classroom is but a shell until it is filled with children. I cannot know, in advance, what the children will bring to our class. What are they curious about? What questions do they have? What are their interests and talents? What life experiences will enrich our collective lives and our learn-ing? Just as I bring my own questions and experiences, each child adds a unique self to our community.

This past school year, during our construction unit, I discovered that two children's families were in the midst of having houses built. We became a part of their house-building step by step. Several children showed an intense interest in bridges. I was amazed at their background knowledge on the intricacies of bridge construction. Before long we were all engaged in hands-on activities exploring the dynamics involved in bridge-building.

I also cannot know how we will interact as a community of learn-ers. It takes time to get to know each other and find ways to accommodate each other's needs. Some children eagerly embrace group experiences while others prefer to work alone. Children learn how to seek each other out—who can help edit, who is fun to read with. Building a community centers around trust—trust in ourselves and in each other.

Finally, I cannot plan what will happen in the world around us that will touch our lives and create "teachable moments"—places where the meaning generated in the classroom bridges the meaning children need in order to understand their community, their universe. Moments such as these engage us in the most authentic kind of learning and connect us in a way that nothing else can.

It was the devastating earthquake in Kobe, Japan, that provided a harsh frame of reference for us last year. We were just beginning to think about constructions, building on what we had discovered about rocks and the forces that shape our earth. Many children brought in newspapers and photographs to share and learn from. The room was abuzz with conversations about how, in this case, the forces of nature were at odds with the building of man.

In my role as teacher I make decisions thinking specifically about the children in my charge, often using science content to point us in a direction that supports a particular constellation of values. Even when I don't actively plan, those values shape our agenda. For instance, I seriously consider how differences in students' backgrounds distance the children from one another. During our construction unit, knowing that all but a few of my students live in affluent, suburban homes, I actively avoided comparisons of the types of shelters students live in. Instead we looked at the many types of dwellings used around the world and thought about how people utilize their natural resources for construction. Last year many of the students would have gladly traded in their houses, regardless of whether they were sprawling colonials or subsidized townhouses, just for the chance to live in a yurt.

In terms of community building I believe students must have choices in terms of how and when they work together. Cooperative learning techniques that have been touted as the solution to a whole host of problems in schools are no substitute for the development of an authentic classroom community. When we were building bridges some students chose to work together, some alone. Some chose to take turns getting materials, others had designated roles within their group. The students worked out their arrangements based on their needs, but we all took an interest in each others work, shared our strategies, and celebrated our accomplishments.

Though many teachable moments present themselves throughout the year, I have to decide which to ignite and which to neglect. In the midst of our construction unit last year, the tragic Oklahoma City bombing caught the attention of the students. Though this event presented obvious real-world construction (or deconstruction) issues, I decided that it was an inappropriate example and subject for six- and seven-year-old children. Though several children continued to bring it up during our morning meetings, I encouraged those children to discuss the tragedy with their families, many of whom were federal employees. On a matter such as this I knew I had to trust my instincts and experience.

> Now I knew what I wanted to say to the pre-service students. All the planning and preparation we do as teachers is important. It's impossible to build without thinking about materials and having the necessary tools. We sketch out a blueprint, a framework of curriculum and routines that will support us throughout the year. What makes each classroom unique, though, is the building process, students and teacher, that takes place throughout the year. Perhaps I was wrong to think of the materials that we bring with us as bricks and mortar. What we bring needs to be far more flexible. The teachers I most admire are those who value their students' questions and make time for their confusion. They are the teachers that build from a foundation of trust and what they create with their students is an authentic reflection of their shared journey.

## Bibliography

Galdone, P. 1973. *The Three Billy Goats Gruff.* New York: Seabury Press.

Gibbons, G. 1990. *How a House Is Built.* New York: Holiday House.

Knight, M.B. 1992. *Talking Walls.* Gardiner, ME: Tilbury House.

Marshall, J. 1989. *The Three Little Pigs*. New York: Dial Books.

Robbins, K. 1991. *Bridges*. New York: Dial Books.

# 9 Carol Flicker

# A Year in the Life of a First-Grade Class

When I think about teaching, I begin with an idea that might seem abstract: I want children to know that, finally, it is their own questions that drive the learning process. In evaluating the activities that take place in my classroom I return again and again to this as a standard. I watch and listen: Do my students see their questions as valuable and welcome? Does it feel safe to offer a guess? Have students developed the analytical skills that enable them to tackle tough problems in writing? In reading? In science? In math?

There are at least two obvious ways to help children learn. In many classrooms teachers build or rely on what would be equivalent to a series of educational locks and dams. Students, in this case, move along a predetermined waterway. When they get stuck the teacher manipulates the learning environment, raises or lowers the water level and allows them to proceed. My class, in contrast, feels like a natural stream that meanders, but ultimately puts children in charge of their own learning and their own destiny. I believe that they leave my class and our school confident that they have the skills to traverse any natural landscape.

8:10 A.M. and the bell has rung. I hear the children pounding down the hallway, an anxious group of first-grade scientists. They rush into the room, eager to check their experiments and observe the animals even before taking off their coats or backpacks. Excitement fills the air as they share with each other the changes that have taken place overnight.

This enthusiasm for learning confirms what I began to observe several years ago. In order to be first-grade scientists, students don't have to know how to read, write, or compute math facts. Given the freedom to explore, observe, question, and experiment, children enjoy science. Curiosity is their greatest ally.

Two years ago I introduced my science program at my school's open house. The Friday morning before school opened all of the students and their families were invited to visit their new classroom homes. I had always found this open house a difficult time. Many first- and second-grade students are apprehensive about what the new school year will bring and somewhat frightened or shy about meeting their new teacher. Their parents are also apprehensive—and curious and concerned. The logistics of setting everyone at ease was always difficult. My main objective was to help the children relax and make them eager to come to school the following week.

Now, after greeting each family, I show the children their desks and invite them to look around the room. Then I walk them to a table on which I had set out an empty ten-gallon fish tank with a sign that reads, "Guess what could live here?" On the table are lots of books and pictures of animals, various kinds of paper, writing implements, and an empty container marked "Guesses." I invite each student to look at the books and pictures, look carefully at the tank, and then draw a picture or write their guesses on a piece of paper. My only hint: It is not a mouse because I'm afraid of mice. I tell them it's OK to make more than one guess and that when they come back next week we will look at the guesses together and see if they can figure out what will really live in the tank. Not only does this make the children eager to come back so they can help solve the mystery, but it also suggests to them that here in school it's OK to take risks when answering a question. And there's an added benefit: This activity gives me a few extra minutes to talk to parents and answer their questions.

Sometime during the first day of school we sit on the floor and discuss what a scientist is:

Someone who is curious about things.
Someone who observes things carefully.
Someone who uses what he knows, what he thinks, and what other
      people think to answer his questions.

I explain that in science there is not always a right or wrong answer to a question and that sometimes scientists can't find the answers to their questions, such as why dinosaurs disappeared.

I suggest that we think like scientists while we look at the guesses. We go through the guesses, putting aside those animals we agree could not possibly live in a tank, usually because of their size. Then I give them additional information—our animal does not live in water. Again we go through the pile, taking out all of the aquatic animals. We are still left with several possibilities. Finally, the children conclude that they need more information. I give them more information, one piece at a time. This enables them to eliminate other guesses. We then set up the tank. When all is ready, I bring out the hermit crabs.

This is the beginning of a year-long unit, the study and care of hermit crabs. We use books, videos, the children's past experiences, and our own observations to learn all we can. In addition to giving the hermit crabs food and water we try a variety of experiments. We take them out of the tank and observe them on the floor, outside on the pavement, and in the grass. We try a variety of foods to see what they really like to eat. Findings are recorded on a class chart, as well as individually in science journals.

After modeling for several days the children are ready to write and illustrate their observations, questions, and ideas individually in journals.

One year we began our science writing by compiling a class book. Each day we would write a sentence about the hermit crabs. I would make a copy for each child to read and illustrate. As we added new pages we always reread the previous ones. At the end of a week each student had a book to take home and share with their family. For many this was an introduction to reading.

Toward the end of September the teacher next door commented that it sounded as if I were teaching science all day long. I realized that she was right. My students were curious, enthusiastic young scientists, eager to question, explore, experiment, observe, research, and record, and I was using science and science books rather than fictional literature to introduce concepts.

But I was still unsure of how much control to give up. Would I be able to plan around the students' interests, I wondered? And I worried that I might miss some of the skills and strategies students needed to acquire in first grade. But the children were so enthusiastic; how could I relegate science to a couple of hours a week? With the encouragement and support of several colleagues I decided to try implementing the Fairfax County Curriculum Guide, using science as the vehicle.

## Research and Observation

One day my student Courtney asked if she could bring in her garter snake, Jack, for sharing. It would be in a tank with a lid, her mother assured me. I agreed. We were fascinated and wanted to learn more about snakes. Courtney told us that her snake was about twenty-five inches long. Together we discussed the difference between twenty-five inches and twenty-five feet. We then took twelve-inch rulers and some chalk outside to measure twenty-five feet. Someone figured out that since there were twenty-two children in our class, each would lay the ruler down once and three people would have more than one turn. Spontaneously math became a part of science lessons. At the end of the day we persuaded Courtney's mother to let us keep the snake in our room for several weeks. She told us that it only ate once a month and had just eaten so we should give it only water.

I gathered all the books I could find on snakes and our research began. A class favorite was Seymour Simon's *Snakes*. They listened to and tried to read the snake books again and again. They became discriminating readers, preferring realistic photographs to illustrations.

We charted the information we learned about snakes on large pieces of paper. I began to notice that many of the children were writing about snakes during writing workshop, utilizing information gathered from reading or observation. After about ten days, Jack was taken home. Courtney promised to bring him back again when it was time for his next feeding.

One day Garrett's mother came in with their black rat snake, Squeezer. Garrett explained that the snake was given his name because of the way he ate. Live mice were put in the tank and then the snake squeezed them to death before eating them. Squeezer, too, lived in a large aquarium with a lid. This second snake simply increased the children's desire to research the topic and compare the two snakes we had observed.

Finally, one morning Courtney's family brought Jack and twelve feeder fish back. The fish were put in a small bowl of water inside the tank and we sat around waiting for the snake to eat. Now we had the two snakes in the room. Trying to keep our thoughts and questions in our heads was going to be difficult. I explained to the children that scientists keep journals where they write about the things they observe, questions they have, and possible answers so that they don't lose track of their thoughts. The children agreed that we should begin to record our ideas in journals. I carefully explained the kinds of things a scientist might put in her journal, including illustrations of her observations. I modeled how to write entries for several days and they quickly caught on and began to write on their own. I noticed that they worked much more independently when they wrote in their science journals than when they did other kinds of writing.

Watching Jack eat his monthly meal provided mathematical opportunities as well as science and language arts lessons. The students kept track of the number of fish in the aquarium, figuring how many fish Jack had eaten that day, how many he had eaten all together, and how many had jumped out of the bowl. During the week that the fish were in Jack's tank, several of them found their way out of their bowl, leading to several excellent discussions and theories as to how the fish got out of the bowl. Had they jumped, or had Jack picked them up and then for some reason dropped them before he ate them? The children based their theories on where in the aquarium the fish were found.

One day Garrett's mom brought in a live baby mouse for Squeezer to eat. At the end of the day when she came to pick up Squeezer, we were all relieved that he hadn't eaten the mouse. Jack also left the same day without having eaten all of his fish. The students' final entry in their snake journals was a comparison of the two snakes. Many wrote that they liked Jack better because they didn't like the fact that Squeezer strangled his food before he ate it.

## Experimentation and Observation

One evening I opened the cupboard under my sink to get some potatoes and decided to bring them to school the next day when I discovered they had begun to sprout. Surprisingly, the children had never seen or noticed the eyes on a potato before and became very excited when I explained that the eyes were the seeds from which new potatoes grow. Everyone had an idea about how the seeds should be planted, and immediately wanted to experiment. Since we did not have enough potatoes, we decided to cut them into pieces. A lively discussion followed about how to cut the potatoes so that each child would have a piece with an eye to experiment with.

Unlike our experiences with the snakes and hermit crabs, where we read lots of books, the children were not at all interested in hearing other scientists' ideas and experiments about potatoes. Clearly, they preferred to experiment on their own.

The fun began. Everyone came up with and shared their ideas about planting. I provided clear plastic containers and soil and let them proceed without giving them any information. Instead I gave them the time and materials to pursue their experiments and the encouragement they needed to try out their ideas. Several students planted their seeds in soil and put them in the cupboard under the sink in our room. They believed that since the potatoes had sprouted under the sink in my house, they would grow better there. Others planted their seeds in soil and put them in closets and under tables. Several tried putting their experiments in the refrigerator and freezer in the teachers' lounge (with notes telling people not to eat them or throw them out). One child said he wanted to plant his in water with toothpicks. My guess is that he had seen a plant in water where toothpicks were used to support it. However, he just stuck his potato in the container of water and stuck all the toothpicks on the top of the potato.

Ashley wanted to put her experiment in the hermit crab's cage. She believed that the aquarium light would act as the sun and make it grow faster. Some of the students were concerned. They were afraid the crab might try to eat the potato and get sick. So Ashley rigged up a cover for her plant, poked holes in it so the plant could get air, securely taped the lid to the container and placed it in the hermit crab tank. Very few students put their seeds in soil and left them in a sunny spot in the room. The few that did overwatered them. Several students wrote notes to remind themselves to check or water their plants. They hung the notes near our class calendar, on their desks, or on the containers with their plants. Again there was a need to organize ideas and record observations in science journals.

Each child began a potato journal to record his experiments, theories, and observations. After several days we gathered on the floor with our experiments for an "All Hands" meeting (this was what we called a science meeting that everyone in the class participated in). Children discussed what was happening to their plants and we made a class chart of our observations. Every morning the children ran into the classroom to check and adjust their plants. One morning Courtney examined hers with a magnifying glass and discovered it was growing roots.

Another day during an All Hands meeting someone discovered that by placing one magnifying glass on top of another the magnification was increased. It was a perfect opportunity to introduce microscopes. The children were fascinated, and all lined up to see mold, scraped from a potato plant, under the lens. They found other things they wanted to observe. Many of them learned how to make their own slides.

Sarah dug her potato up, discovered it had gotten very hard, and wondered why. Rosie said it was because the water had evaporated. This led to a discussion and several experiments on water evaporation, a concept they understood and referred to throughout the rest of the year.

Within a month all but one of the plants had died or never sprouted.

We made a class chart listing why we thought our experiments failed. Joshua decided that the ones in the freezer and refrigerator didn't grow because it was too cold in there. He learned that plants need warmth to grow. Other children realized they had overwatered their plants. Some of the children believed their plants might still grow. Then Courtney shared her experiment. Hers was the only plant that was growing. Courtney's had grown so large she thought she should move it to another container. We discussed the word transplant. It became one of the children's favorite science words. Most of the children learned how to spell it; it was easy to sound out.

The information on our chart helped us to realize what we might have done wrong in our initial experiments. Everyone wanted to try again. I read them several pages from *The Great Potato Book* by Meredith Sayles Hughes and E. Thomas Hughes, which explained in detail how to plant potato seeds. Fortunately, a parent donated a bag of sprouting potatoes. Using the information we had learned from our first experiments and from our reading, we tried again.

We began with a math lesson on problem solving. We counted the number of potatoes we had and the number of eyes each potato had, and then figured out how to cut the potatoes so that each person had at least one piece to experiment with. (These first graders were not just adding and subtracting, but were multiplying and dividing.) The children were determined to make these experiments work. Some reread the directions on how to plant the seeds and followed them exactly. They worked with a friend to make sure they planted their seeds in the recommended amount of soil at the proper depth. They were much more careful about the amount of water they gave their plants. Instead of putting the plants in the sink and turning on the faucet they came up with ideas to better control the amount of water their plants received. Someone decided to fill a cup with water and then pour it on the plant; another began to use a squirt bottle; yet another began wetting a sponge and wringing it out over the plant. Many of the students placed their plants in a dark place, believing that if my potatoes sprouted in the dark, theirs would too. Others found sunny places in the classroom for their plants. After several days many of the plants sprouted. The students were thrilled and anxious to share their results. We called an All Hands meeting. With plants in hand they sat in a large circle on the floor. One of the things they discovered was that the plants that had been in the dark had white sprouts while those that had been exposed to the light had green sprouts. The children concluded that although plants sprouted in the dark, they needed the light to remain healthy.

## Procedure

Our All Hands meeting evolved into a three-step process that often lasted several hours. We began by sitting in a circle and sharing our experiments, theories, and what we planned to do next. During the second part of the meeting each student had the opportunity to walk around and closely observe their peers' experiments and care for their own plants. They used that time to transplant, stake, add more soil, measure, examine their plants more closely with a magnifying glass, or look at something under a microscope. Before beginning the third part of our science activity, journal writing, we would discuss some of the things they might include in their journal. I usually taught a mini-lesson on punctuation, spelling, or grammar at this time. Then they would take out their science journals, write the date using the numerical code and proceed, documenting their observations, actions, and ideas. I encouraged them to work without my help, reviewing each time, before they wrote, a variety of strategies they could use when they needed help. For instance, if they got stuck on spelling a word they could sound it out, look for it on a chart or in a book or dictionary, or they could ask a friend. As a last resort, they could ask me. I would help them to sound the word out as well as find them the correct spelling. My own time could then be used mostly for writing conferences and small group mini-lessons.

I believe that potatoes themselves were not the key to the unit's success. The key was giving my students the time to observe their plants, try out their ideas, and ask questions, allowing their interests and skills to develop naturally.

## Curricular Integration

As our plants began to grow the children realized they would need to find a way to measure their growth. Initially they used twelve-inch rulers from our math kit; however, as the plants grew, many of them bent, or grew longer than twelve inches. Yardsticks were too cumbersome to use. Cloth tape measures seemed to be the best choice. The only drawback was that the measurements were in centimeters instead of inches. The children quickly discovered the approximate size difference in the units of measurement, and enjoyed reporting their results because of the "bigger numbers." The week before spring vacation I noticed a student putting Scotch tape along the top of his plant. He explained that by putting tape around the plant, he thought that he would be able to quickly see how much it had grown while we were on vacation. It worked!

Soon I began to notice a difference in the quality of the students' writing and in their ability to work independently when they were doing science journals. During science writing no one ever said, "I don't know what to write about today," or "I don't want to write." Moreover, they rarely asked me for help, instead trying to find words themselves or with a friend. To facilitate their efforts with a dictionary, I taught them how to alphabetize words. Then I gave each student a *Journeys Writing Dictionary*. These paperback books are consumable, and each letter has several words already entered and several blank pages for students to add words of their own. Although the printed words are alphabetized, the students' entries are only alphabetized to the first letter; my first graders found them very easy to use. After becoming familiar with these dictionaries, some of the students wanted to use the "big" dictionary. In small group mini-lessons, I introduced the strategies they would need to locate words. Their ability to work on their own during science writing allowed me the opportunity to conduct small group and individual conferences and mini-lessons.

The children's journal entries enabled me to assess many of their skills and helped me plan future focus lessons. I was amazed at the content of their entries. The observations and comparisons they made were accurate and informative. I noted with pride that even the weakest students were putting effort into their writing.

Planting the potatoes in clear plastic containers enabled the children to watch the root system grow. They decided that it was time to transplant their sprouts when the roots reached the bottom of the container and began to grow upward. Unfortunately, I could not find any large, inexpensive, clear containers, but the children didn't seem to mind. I began buying potting soil, and by the end of the year I had purchased about two hundred pounds of it! Many of the children's plants were now in buckets so large that they were unable to move them by themselves, so we had to enlist the help of the sixth-grade boys across the hall. It was important to the first graders that no matter how big or heavy their plants became, they were able to bring them to our All Hands meetings.

One day, Courtney carefully dug a hole next to her plant and discovered a small potato! The excitement was contagious, and the entire class became even more eager to continue their experiments.

   The plants, and the class' enthusiasm, continued to thrive. Parents, other teachers, and visitors came by to see and hear about our plants. As the end of the school year approached, I began to wonder about what to do with the potato plants. None of the children wanted to get rid of their plants, but most were too large to be carried home in their containers.

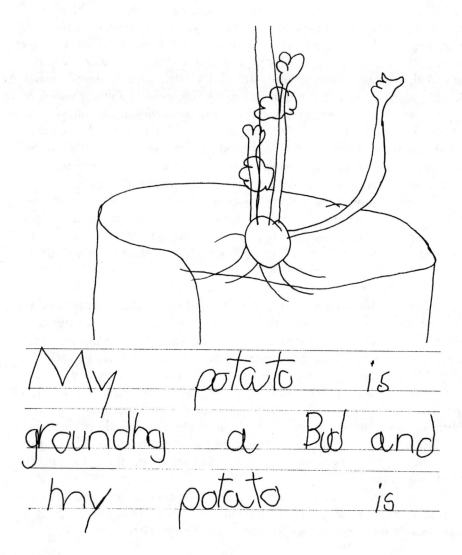

**FIGURE 9–1**

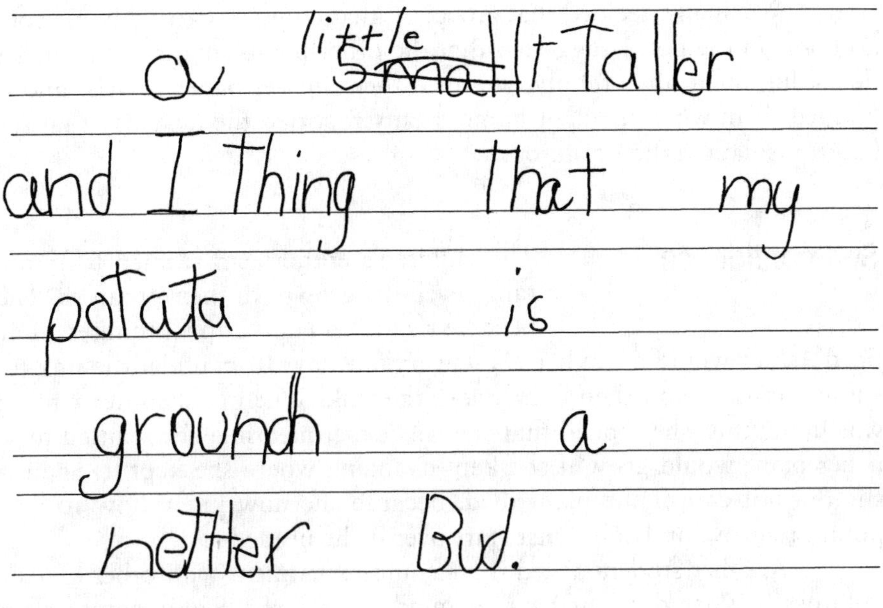

a little ~~small~~ It Taller
and I thing that my
potata is
grounch a
hetter Bud.

FIGURE 9–1 *(continued)*

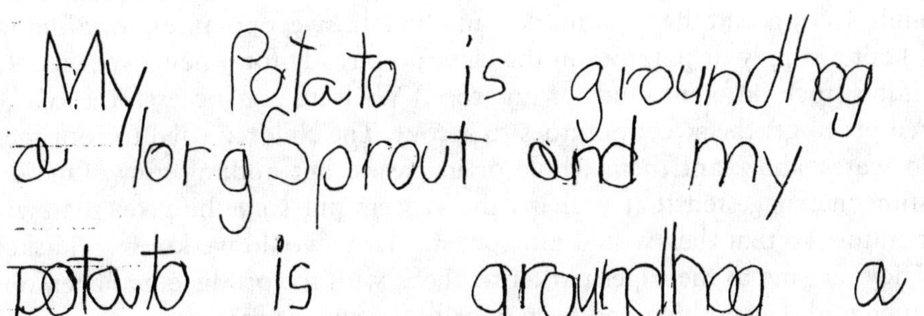

My Potato is groundhog
a longSprout and my
potato is groundhog a
little potato and my
potato is groundhog a
long rat

FIGURE 9–2

We finally decided that any plant that could be carried home could go home in the pot. I suggested that the other plants might live if the students dug them up carefully, wrapped them in wet paper towels, and replanted them when they got home. Many reported the next day that they had transplanted their potatoes.

## Self-confidence

The children's enthusiasm seemed to outdistance even the growth of their potatoes. They became risk-takers and critical thinkers. I noticed Ashley would move her plant every few days from under the sink to a sunny location, and then back under the sink. When I asked her why she was doing this, she replied that she was experimenting; she wanted to see if her plant would grow if she kept changing where she kept it. She said she did not care if the plant died, because she now knew how to get a potato to grow, and could just start over if she needed to.

Another student asked if we could experiment with other kinds of potatoes. "What did you have in mind?" I asked. "Sweet potatoes and mashed potatoes" was his reply. We decided we would experiment with sweet potatoes, and discussed why mashed potatoes would not grow. (That night I stopped at the supermarket and bought sweet potatoes, for although I kept a supply of potatoes in the classroom ready for a new experiment, I didn't stock different kinds of potatoes.) We were not successful in our attempts to get the sweet potatoes to sprout. The children tried to root them in water, and plant them whole or in pieces, but nothing grew. One day someone suggested that perhaps the grocers put something on the sweet potatoes so that they would not sprout. "How would we know?" I asked. They sent me to the supermarket to check with the produce manager, only to be told that nothing had been done to the sweet potatoes.

Another time I purchased potatoes from two different supermarkets one day apart. When all of the potatoes from one supermarket sprouted before any from the other market, the children decided that the produce in one supermarket was fresher than in the other.

One of the children in my class could neither read nor write intelligibly. He still did not recognize all the letters in the alphabet, but loved anything to do with science; he brought in turtles, frogs, and his pet rabbit to share with us. He took great pride in his potato plant and cared for it every day. In fact, one day Mr. Mehm, our principal, said that this student had told him, "I'm one of the best scientists in my class because my potato is growing so well. I take good care of it."

I called the Fairfax County Agriculture Information extension service to get information on planting potatoes and was told that the idea was ridiculous. You could not grow potatoes indoors in containers because they needed room to grow. When I reported back to the children they were not deterred. They saw themselves as scientists conducting an experiment, and no one knew what would happen until they tried.

One day the children noticed I had removed several science charts from the room. I explained that I was going to talk to a group of teachers and wanted to share some of the class' ideas and discoveries. They said OK, but I had to promise to tell them what the teachers said. They questioned me the next day.

> **Student:** What did the teachers think of our charts and journals?
> **Teacher:** They said I must have a smart class.
> **Student:** Of course we're smart.
> **Teacher:** The teachers wondered how first graders could be scientists.
> **Student:** We have brains, we can think.
> **Teacher:** The teachers wanted to know when we do reading and math.
> **Student:** We read, write, and do math when we need to and when we want to.

The students were indignant that teachers would question their seriousness of purpose and a lively discussion followed.

## Assessing the Year

As the year drew to a close I decided to evaluate my "experiment." I sat down with the Fairfax County Curriculum Guide, the students' writings, my journal, and my observations and evaluations of the students' work, and thought back to my initial concern: "If I used science as the vehicle, could I successfully teach the skills and strategies delineated in the Fairfax County Curriculum Guide?" With satisfaction, I realized all of the objectives had been covered in real and meaningful ways.

In language arts the students learned to:

work in small groups
ask questions to explore a topic
discuss ideas for reading and
    writing
share ideas, materials, and work
locate information
distinguish fact from fiction
recall knowledge
use multiple strategies to attach
    meaning to print

follow directions
take turns
form opinions about content (they
    developed preferences for
    certain authors and preferred
    photographs to illustrations in
    science books)
experiment with words
initiate ideas for reading and
    writing

In math they learned:

how to use standard units of
    measurement, both inches and
    centimeters
the days of the week, months, and
    time to the half hour
addition
subtraction

the concept of division
the concept of multiplication
estimation
how to analyze data
number concepts
geometry
problem solving

In social studies they learned:

how to acquire, process, apply, and share information
about families and communities; we used our animals and their
    communities and then studied our own families and community

By the end of the school year, all of the students were attempting to write in their science journals independently. Although not all were reading on grade level, evaluations by the reading teacher showed they had the proper strategies in place. Most important, they were all inquisitive, enthusiastic learners. They had developed self-confidence and were eager to read, listen, and question written material, their peers, and even adults.

As I read through my journal I came across several observations that proved to me that the year had been a success. I thought of those children for whom reading and writing remained a challenge. One child who had a speech impediment and frequent hearing problems due to ear infections came to mind. He had difficulty identifying letter sounds, and even at the end of the year his reading and spelling skills were weak. But this boy loved snakes, and read and reread Seymour Simon's snake book. In fact, whenever anyone else wanted the book they knew to check with him first. One morning I noticed this student on the floor intently studying the book. I watched him examine a picture of a snake and its tracks, then curl his body up, throw his head back, and try to move his body like the snake in the picture. He repeated this movement, changing his body slightly each time, until he was satisfied with the result. It was clear that he had found a book that mattered to him.

Another day I observed a mentally impaired student who had been mainstreamed into my room looking at the same book. He called a friend over and asked him to explain something in the text. The friend, who was a nonreader, sat down, and watched his classmate turn the pages from left to right instead of right to left. He said, "You're reading it wrong. If you read it the right way you'll know what it says," and showed him the correct way to turn the pages.

The mainstreamed student was an eight-year-old who came from a program for the minimally mentally retarded. Gradually he began to spend more and more time with our class, although he spoke very little and never participated in group discussions. He recognized the letters of the alphabet and some consonant sounds, but could not read or write anything independently. Still, he enjoyed experimenting. By the end of the year he was reading on a beginning first-grade level and writing several sentences without my help. As he realized that risk-taking was encouraged and everyone's ideas were respected, he started to participate in group discussions and activities.

## The Inquiring Mind

About a week after school ended I received the first in a series of letters from Rosie. In the letters she described to me what was happening to her potato plant.

In September she came back to visit every few days and to report on the plant's progress. She had decided to wait until the plant died before digging to see if any potatoes had grown. One October morning, eager to share her results, she stopped by. She had dug up her plant the previous afternoon and found several little potatoes. But she was not going to eat them; they were for experimenting.

Another morning Courtney came by with several small potatoes

Dear Mrs. Flicker,
As I side I would, I planted
my potato. It used to be 4 in,
now it's 6! The othr one
used to be 1 now it's 1"½.
the othr one used to be
      below the ground and
now it's ½. (You will
be geting a lot of the
se lett ers.)

    Dear Mrs. Flicker,

    My potato seems to like

the heat. It grows all
the more in this wedther
I is 23 in. It grew 10 in. in ½
week!

    PS. You know how buds on
a potato are little round
spikey things? Well I don't
know if its the heat or the or the
kind of potato but the kind of
bud I have looks like In pa tient
buds. I have 13. the flower is
white with a yellow middle.

**FIGURE 9–3**

she had harvested. "And there were even more," she reported, "though I left the little ones in the ground to see if they would grow into tater tots™!"

Am I going to introduce sprouting potatoes again next year? I am not sure. The potatoes were simply an inexpensive and easily acquired material that allowed us the luxury of trial and error. If we had experimented with more scarce or expensive materials, the children and I would have been less willing to take risks. I found it useful to make a list of inexpensive readily available things that might spark a young scientist's interest.

## Follow-up

Although we have researched and experimented with different things each year, science continues to play a dominant role in my classroom. My students think and act like scientists. Their interest and enthusiasm for the "real world" has enabled them to read, write, and problem solve beyond their years. They continue to learn to ask questions, take risks, and work cooperatively.

As for me, I feel more convinced than ever that all children are interested in science, but not always in the same aspects of science. So once I have laid the groundwork on how to think and act like a scientist, I no longer ask that each student study or research the same topic. I listen carefully to what the children say and what books interest them, and try to provide guidance and materials to help them pursue their interests. Our sixth-grade neighbors have sometimes helped us with research and compiling our information, and in exchange we have shared our knowledge about the animals and plants in our room with them. In fact, last year several sixth graders were taught how to use a microscope by their first-grade friends.

Using readily available materials, students have enjoyed learning about various aspects of the real world. We dried flowers from a bouquet a student brought in last fall and planted the flowers in the spring. We took the seeds from a sunflower and planted them. Three classes planted acorns under a variety of conditions and then compared how each group's plants progressed. We studied pumpkins and planted their seeds. We have had two different kinds of pet toads. A sixth-grade class gave us some mealworms last winter and we spent several months researching, observing, and experimenting with them as they changed. First-grade students have learned about the ocean and have done experiments with water, including making salt water, growing crystals, and coloring solutions. This year we have two Venus's-flytrap plants. The children are fascinated by their eating habits. Each year I have begun my science program at open house. The hermit crabs I introduce have helped the students learn to think, observe, and record data as scientists do.

Much of my teaching has changed over the past several years, and that is at once exciting and frightening. At first it was difficult to give up some of my control and let the children's interests guide our days, but I am convinced this is what made the difference. Now I watch and listen to my students, respond to their interests, and allow them time to experiment. Together we work in a community, learners all.

## Bibliography

Simon, Seymour. 1992. *Snakes*. New York: HarperCollins Publishers.

Hughes, Meredith Sayles, and E. Thomas Hughes. 1986. *The Great Potato Book*. New York: Macmillan Publishing Co.

Hollaway, Judith. 1989. *Journeys Writing Dictionary*. Canada: Ginn Publishing.

# 10 Jeanne Reardon

# Consumer Testing: Children Working on Authentic Science Problems

This chapter grows from experiences during my second year using a workshop approach to science learning. The first year we had truly become a community of scientists (see Reardon 1993, for a detailed discussion), and I was curious to see how another year would work. I was particularly interested in the events and questions that led children to their own science investigations. This was a combination first- and second-grade class with fifteen first-grade children and eleven in second grade. Five of the second graders had been with me the year before and were eager for Science Workshop to begin.

During our first year using a science workshop we confronted many problems as we explored and investigated. Often these were the same kinds of problems encountered by adult scientists—problems that arise in the practice of science. There were problems that focused on bringing something into the laboratory to study more closely as opposed to keeping it in its natural environment. "How can we look at raindrops in our room?" we asked. "Will the materials that repel water in our room repel rain outside?" There were questions of accuracy and recording: "Did you wait just as long as last time?" Challenges with testing to confirm explanations also presented themselves: "You said wood is a magnet for water. How can you tell?"; "Show me what you mean, *pull* water drops with a Popsicle™ stick"; "You used newsprint for this test and construction paper for . . ." There were also "how to" problems: "How can I keep the cloth from falling into the cup when I drop water on it?"

The questions, challenges, and discussions during our Scientists' Meetings (Reardon, 1993, 28) often focused on the problems children encountered during their scientific quests. I noticed that children came to these scientists' problems quite naturally during their work, but I kept wondering, Are there some events, situations, or questions that children identify as "science" problems? Do six- and seven-year-old children encounter science problems, or just problems? Being unable to figure out if Nick really took too long a turn at the easel is a mathematics problem—we can use mathematics to solve it. Not understanding the written directions to the game is a reading problem. But what about the paint that keeps dripping down the paper on the easel? Do the children see it as a science problem, an art problem, or just a problem? Maybe they are all just problems with different kinds of solutions—reading, math, and science solutions.

## Listening for Children's Science Problems

It would be helpful to me to know an authentic child science problem when I meet one, but it is not always easy to recognize what will develop into a science inquiry or problem for a child. And so I keep asking, "What are the science concerns children meet in their daily lives? What are the issues that require an understanding of science and of the ways scientists work? Which call for a scientific judgment? Which are really adult issues and which are child issues?" These were my questions as I watched, listened, and worked with children throughout the day.

Often we work to find meaningful ways of bringing adult science problems to children. We adults are concerned with the environmental issues of pollution, use of dwindling natural resources, and disposal of wastes, so we celebrate Earth Day with our class. We help children reuse and recycle, we measure amounts of trash accumulated at home and at school, we bury trash and later dig it up, and many children come to share our concerns. This is valuable, but is it a "kid problem"? I know that children who select their own books and topics and reflect on their own experiences while reading and writing become lifetime readers and writers. I believe that children who investigate their own science problems in the classroom will become lifetime scientists. And so I began the year wondering about the children's science problems. This chapter describes one way that we, the children and I, came to recognize and work with our own authentic science problems. (See the Appendix for examples of other children's science problems we have studied.)

It was my personal use of *Consumer Reports* magazine that helped me listen differently for science problems in our classroom. I routinely look to *Consumer Reports* when I am considering a major purchase, but more often I browse through the magazine noting the strengths and weaknesses of the products tested and comparing the test findings with my own experience. "That's it!" I thought. "Children are consumers and they recognize product problems." I could see the science happening in our classroom: Consumer testing would bring together concepts of science, the processes of science, scientific ways of thinking, and applications of science. Now I had a new way to listen.

## The First-Grade Consumer-Scientist at Work

Our consumer testing activities all have been sparked by both an event and a problem. We have investigated erasers that smear, crumble, or tear paper; books that come apart; adhesive bandages that don't stick; jammed staplers; and playground balls that lose air. What do these things have in common? All are familiar and important parts of kids' lives. That's where our most fruitful science investigations have begun—with problems and materials that are familiar and important to the children.

### The Children's Problem

Our first big product investigation was with wide line markers. It began with a conversation I overheard.

"We gotta find the cap or it'll dry out."

"Some of these markers are dried out, and the caps stick on real tight."

"Yeah, some markers are no good."

"Some of 'em are so wet they go right through the paper!"

During Science Workshop that afternoon I recalled the conversation I had overheard in the morning and our consumer testing of markers was under way. There was an immediate outpouring of marker stories and tales of humor, delight, and frustration. When there was a break in the conversation I asked the children to list the problems they had with markers and characteristics they look for when they choose markers.

We all brought our Scientist's Notebooks and a pencil with us to meetings. (See the Appendix for Scientist's Notebook information.) The children opened their notebooks and wrote headings. I suggested writing "Problems I've had with markers" on one page, and "A really good marker will . . ." on another page. Some children immediately translated my headings to their own—"good stuff" and "bad stuff." I considered telling the class that scientists often thought problems were interesting, not necessarily "bad," but reconsidered and waited. The children's problem lists grew quickly, while the desired characteristics lists grew more slowly.

When working with unfamiliar materials in science, we usually spend a considerable amount of time exploring and messing around before we are ready to write and plan investigations. The children were so familiar with markers that they did not need this exploration time and were ready to write and plan their investigations. I listed all of the problems on a chart, then did the same with desirable characteristics. The children's titles were fitting, and the lists became "good stuff" and "bad stuff." The lists looked like this:

| Bad Stuff | Good Stuff |
|---|---|
| color gets light | lasts a long time |
| cap falls off and gets lost | bright colors |
| goes right through the paper | doesn't go through the paper |
| won't wash off | washes off |
| color runs out—doesn't last | has a place to keep the cap |
| makes streaks | doesn't fade (get light) |
| smells | smells good |
| makes fuzzy, spread-out lines | cap doesn't fall off |
| little "hairs" come out | writing part lasts (does not bend |
| too bendy | or spread out, get fuzzy) |
| tears paper | |

We looked at the lists and noticed that "everything sort of matches," so we made a short list of what we could investigate:

**Investigations**
marker caps
going through paper
running out of color
the part you write with
smells
washing off

When we begin thinking about a product, we make both a problem list and a desirable characteristics list. Usually the lists match, but sometimes they don't. It is easier for children to identify problems than desirable characteristics. Making both lists helps children focus their attention on attributes. It is not easy for young children to narrow their attention—during science, this quality of noticing and wondering about everything can be both an asset and a hindrance. Children frequently make serendipitous discoveries, but miss important details. (Note: Since this is the way six- and seven-year-olds are, we attempt to keep track of as much of our thinking as possible. The children use their journals to note what they observe, what they wonder about, what surprises them, what they understand, and what problems they encounter. These are usually all mixed up. During another part of the day we reread our Scientist's Notebooks, code entries, and discuss them. I keep track of incidental curiosities, questions, and discoveries for later exploration and investigation.)

## Plans and Testing

Children selected the topic they would like to investigate and I put groups together. Color that washes off, color that lasts, caps that stay on, and ink that goes through were the problems selected for investigation. (There were two "color that lasts" groups.) The notion of tests and evidence is not easy for first- and second-grade children. Children often do not see a need to test their ideas and explanations. For many children of this age, "Making a statement makes it so"; they need nothing more to satisfy their sense of evidence. I think of this as the "Saying is believing" school of evidence. I will always remember the child who told me, "I know because I read it in a book—that only children can read." Other children demonstrate high standards for tests and evidence when investigating their own problem/question, but make few demands when the problem is not theirs. In my classroom I have observed that self-selection of investigations affects scientific rigor and students' interest and excitement. Young children discover the need for control variables, replication, accurate measurement, and data recording when the investigation is their own and when their fellow scientists question them.

"Scientists work at many different jobs," I reminded the class during our next workshop. "Some scientists' work is testing products. That is what we are going to do." We talked generally about product testing. The children were aware of the recall of automobiles with unsafe gas tanks. I told them, "You have been hired to test markers like those we use in our room to make the wide lines. We will try out three different brands of markers. You'll need to think about what you can do to test—to find out how well the markers do 'the good stuff.' Let's talk about what makes a test fair."

Seven- and eight-year-old children have a strong sense of fairness and justice. What they describe as fair is what we term control variables. "You gotta start with all new markers. You gotta do the same thing with all of them," the children say.

"Well, what exactly will you do?" I ask. "Get together with your group and come up with some ideas to try out on the rest of us. We'll all talk over your plans. What will you do to see if washable markers are washable?" I ask Vanessa's group. The groups all came up with plans and presented them. Then the questions and suggestions came. Figure 10–1 shows the first testing plan of the "wash off" group.

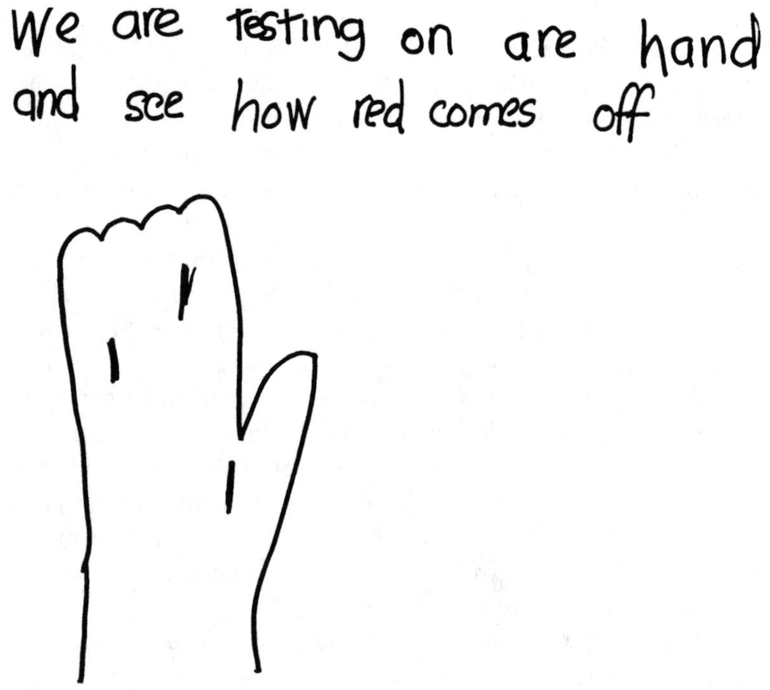

We are testing on are hand
and see how red comes off

FIGURE 10–1

I purchased five sets of three different brands of wide line washable markers. Every day for three weeks the children tested. Usually I set aside forty minutes for testing and thirty minutes for reports of testing in progress, data collections, demonstrations, and discussion. One or two groups would report on their progress, problems, and findings during our Scientists' Meetings each day. All of the children kept records, talked, and borrowed ideas from each other.

## Revising Tests

The group testing to see how well markers washed off frequently revised their tests. This group began by drawing lines on their hands and washing them off. All of the children had experience with marker ink on their skin and clothes. There was high interest whenever the wash off group presented their tests. "What marker made that red line? It never washed off."

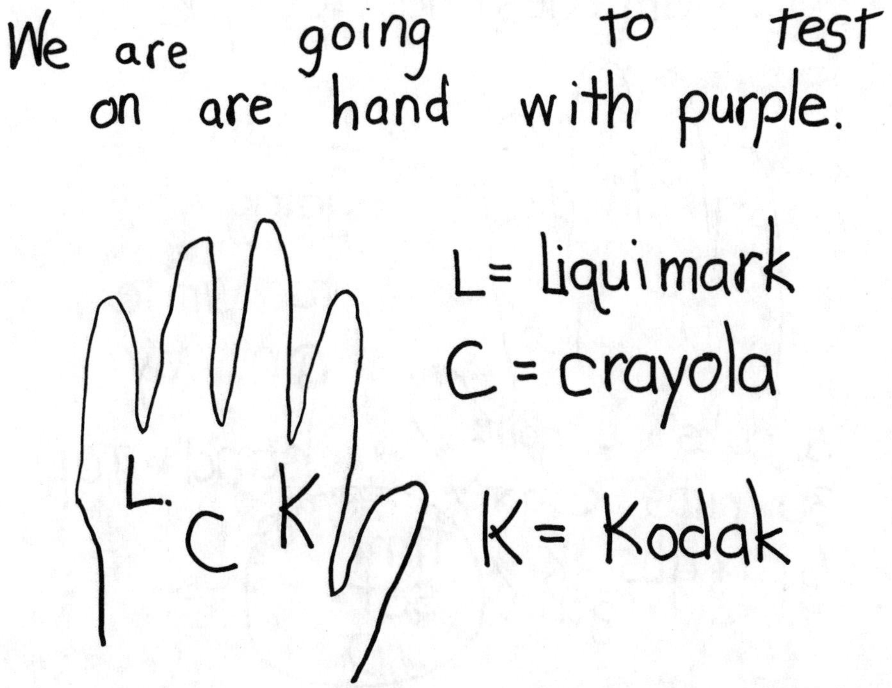

We are going to test on are hand with purple.

L = liquimark
C = crayola
K = Kodak

**FIGURE 10–2**

"How do you know the brand?" "I think it's Crayola™ . . . maybe it's Kodak™ . . ." In order to remember which markers were tested, they wrote the initial letter of each brand name.

After several children had observed variations when different colors were used, the class decided that when they compared brands they should use the same color marker. The wash off group incorporated this into their testing. Following the groups' third presentation at our Scientists' Meeting, the children made several observations and comments. "Nobody goes and washes right away when you get marker on you." "You should wait awhile before you see if it washes off." "You better set the timer."

When questioned about how they washed the marker off their hands, the group further refined their tests. At the end of three weeks their

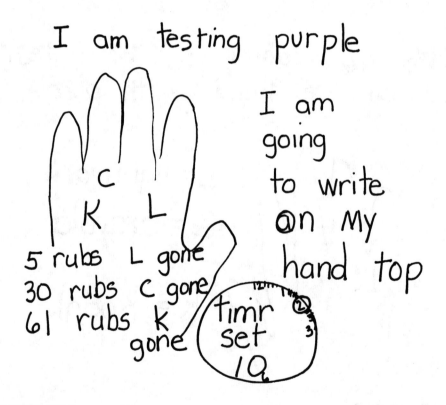

FIGURE 10-3

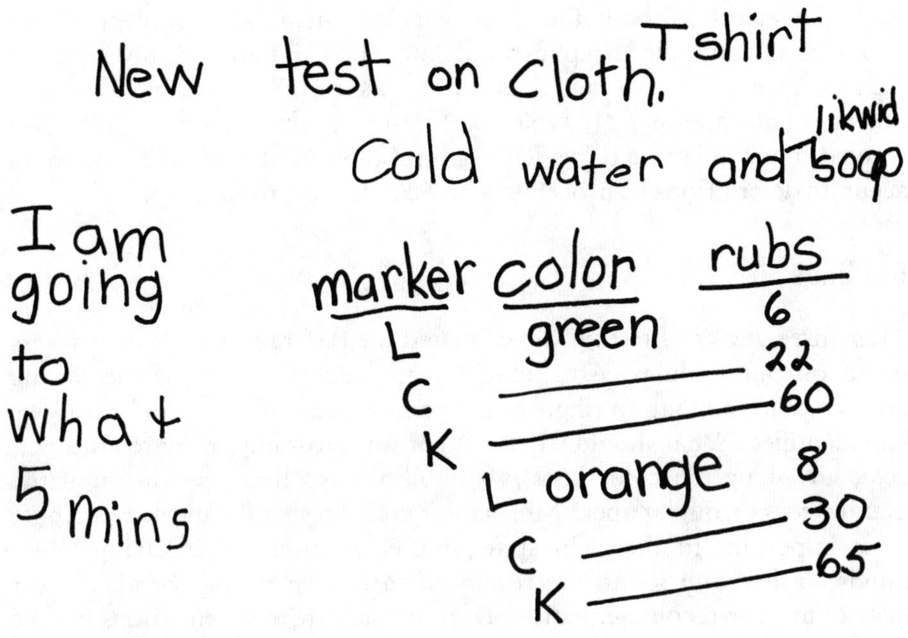

New test on cloth. Tshirt

Cold water and soap likwid

I am
going
to
what
5 mins

marker  color  rubs
  L      green    6
  C              22
  K              60
  L    orange    8
  C              30
  K              65

**FIGURE 10-4**

records showed how many rubs it took to remove each letter made on the top of a hand and left to dry for five minutes. There were tests for red, green, blue, and orange markers from all three brands—tests made with soap and without, under cold water and warm. The group had also made tests to see how markers washed off fabrics.

## Controlling Variables and Replication

The children's control of variables and test refinement came in response to the questions of fellow scientists. Curiosity, interest in the testing group's problem, and a sense of fairness motivated the children's questions. Every child had used markers, and thus had a stake in the problem. I did not teach the children to identify variables or model *the right way* to carry out a scientific experiment. Children who have time to work and meet together to solve their own science problems appear to begin controlling variables on their own.

As I think about the class working on marker problems, I am struck by the amount of replication I saw. The children not only repeated their own tests, but also tried out each other's tests. When the children saw others rolling markers off tables to find out if the caps come off, they wanted to try the same thing. This natural replication of tests led to more accurate descriptions of procedures and careful record keeping.

## Findings

After three weeks of testing we evaluated the different brands of markers based on our findings. After studying the reports of all of the testing groups we found that no single brand combined all of the "good stuff" we had identified. What should we do? What was most important to consider: cost, how long the color lasts, washability, caps that stay on, or if the marker goes through paper? Most children had tested the marker attribute most important to them. In spite of friends' attempts to change their minds, each group found the results of their own testing weighed most heavily in their recommendation. Decisions and recommendations can be more complicated than they first appear. We learned that there may not be one clear answer.

> Finding 1: I think you should get Crayola™ markers because it lasted against Kodak™ and Liqui-mark™. I know because I tested it with my partners. Also probably because it is a good brand.
>
> Finding 2: I think that the school should buy Liqui-mark™ marker. I have reasons. We had tests. 1. The caps barely fall off. 2. It washes off the best. 3. They do not run out very fast and for $1.99 you can get 15.

Although we worked scientifically, science did not tell us which marker brand to buy. Instead we had to consider all of the reports and make our own informed decision.

Initially I had thought we would share our findings with our families, but the class decided that there was a wider audience for our work. They thought that everyone at school would be interested in our recommendation of the best brand of markers, so we displayed our work in the hall outside our room. We included our original charts of "Bad Stuff" and

"Good Stuff," papers describing our tests, record sheets, large data collections, and many individual recommendations. This was the most widely read bulletin board in the school. Fifth-grade students and visitors to the school would stop in to ask questions of the consumer scientists in our room.

## Time for Problem Science and . . .

In this chapter I have written about using children's own science problems to build an understanding of science. Just as not all problems are science problems, there is more to learning science than solving problems. While testing the markers, the children often raised related science questions. Their notebooks contained many questions and observations:

What makes the click when the cap is almost on?
How come some markers squeak? What makes the squeak?
What makes caps stick on when you hold them upside down? How come
        some stuff sticks and some stuff slides—and some rolls?
How does the color keep crawling out after you take the marker away?
        It's just like water color. It crawls faster when the paper is wet.

As teachers, these questions thrill us, but then we pause. How can we help Erica study osmosis, Sam study friction, Becky study sound . . . ? Sometimes children are able to pursue their questions at home. Sometimes I have had all of the children select one of two interest topics and worked with the class on the two topics simultaneously. Often I provide project time for children to pursue special interests, sometimes even getting outside helpers from other classes, the high school, or community to meet with special interest groups. The difficulty I find with children working on many different projects is that we lose the challenging comments and questions that come when the class has a common pursuit. Most often we record questions, and when we meet to reread our Scientist's Notebooks, we talk about them as questions: Where did the question come from? What does the question make you think of? Is it like anything else you know? What could you do to find out more? This discussion recognizes the value of the children's questions and gives them starters for their personal pursuit.

The selection of markers is not one of earth's great problems, but it was a real problem for children in this class. In pursuing marker problems the children began to develop both the skills and attitudes of science. I continue to watch and listen for those events that will become the children's science problems. I believe that we come to understand science best by working through our own problems. This year the children have joined me in looking at problems and asking, "Is this a science problem?"

## Appendix: The Scientist's Notebook

### Setting Up the Notebook

Use legal size, unlined, white duplicating paper (8½″ × 14″). Staple 20–25 sheets together horizontally. Title the front cover, then turn over from bottom to top and write "???? and Plans" on the back cover. Children will work from both ends to the middle of the journal.

### Using the Notebook

Before children make entries in their journal they fold under 1½″–2″ from the right hand edge of the page. This provides space for children to write comments, ideas, explanations, and future explorations when they reread their journals.

### Exploration Time

During exploration time (getting to know the materials, messing about, exploring possibilities) the children stop every ten or fifteen minutes to write what they are doing, what they noticed, what they wonder about, and anything that surprised them. Children use drawings, lists, phrases, sentences, charts, and conversation bubbles to record what they are exploring and thinking.

### Investigation Time

During investigation time (purposeful trying-out, testing, seeking an answer, constructing an explanation) the children record as they work. While the children are investigating I stop by to chat and ask, "How will you record that? What are you writing about that?"

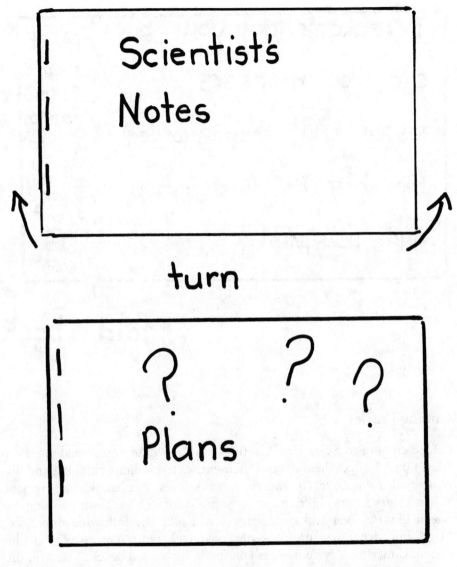

FIGURE 10–5

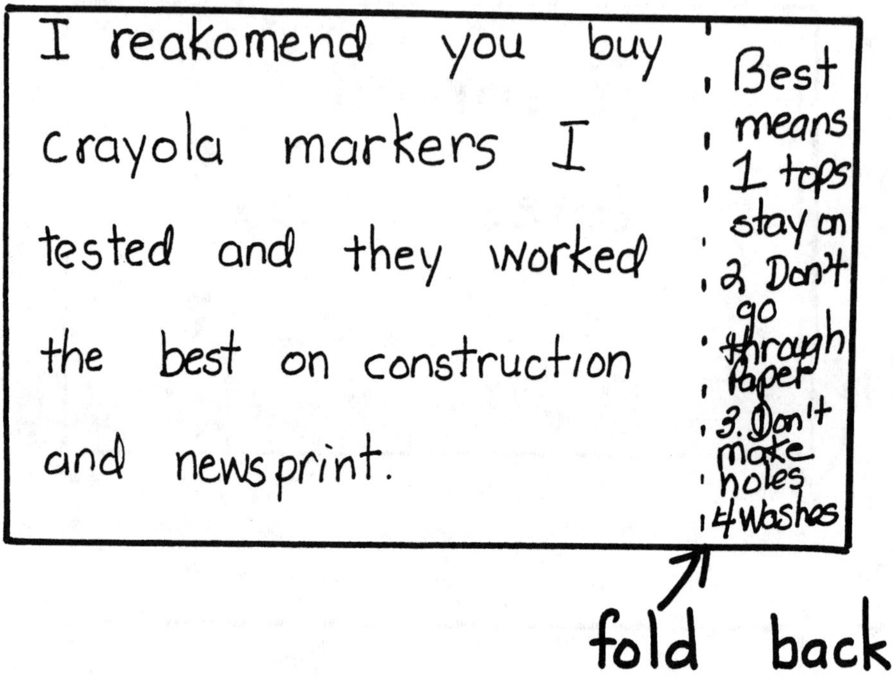

I reakomend you buy crayola markers I tested and they worked the best on construction and news print.

Best means 1 tops stay on 2 Don't go through paper 3. Don't make holes 4 washes

fold back

FIGURE 10–6

## Coding Entries

Before coming to Scientists' Meetings children date and reread their entries. Often I direct them to code their entries to facilitate thinking and discussion. I have children underline procedures, explanations, surprises. When I notice that children are having a difficult time distinguishing between observations and comments, I will give the following directions, "Underline what you noticed—observed with your senses—with a blue pencil. Underline any comments you made with a red pencil." We will discuss both during our meeting, and talk about how comments help to make connections and build explanations while observations.

## A Resource for Discussion

Children bring their notebooks with them to the Scientists' Meetings. During the meetings three to five children report on their work in progress and lead the discussion. Other children offer questions, suggestions, or challenges. After each discussion the children are given time to enter further questions, plans, etc., in their notebooks.

## A Resource for Building Science Understanding

Notebooks are used at other times during the day in small group and whole class lessons to look for implied questions, to plan for or refine testing of hunches, to share ways to find answers to questions, to discuss the significance of surprises, to construct concepts, to settle on common vocabulary, to make connections . . . the list is endless.

# Appendix: Science Problems

## Children's Problems

gluesticks (dry out, won't wind up or wind down, caps won't come off)
erasers (smudge, tear paper, crumble)
tempera paint (cracks off when dry, runs down the paper)
adhesive bandages (don't stick, hurt when they come off)
mittens (Which kind keep your hands warm? Which ones keep your
      hands dry in the snow?)
jackets (Which ones keep you dry in the rain?)
sneakers (Do some really make you run faster or jump higher?)
shoelaces (Which ones—cotton, leather, flat, round—stay tied?)
packaged lunch foods (Which packages are easiest to open? What is the
      best way to get in?)

## Problems in the Practice of Science

These are problems encountered by all working scientists—adult or child.

taking something out of its natural environment to study
record keeping
constructing fair tests
"how to" (construct an apparatus that will do what you need, keep
      fish still to study them, see what is happening inside or
      underground)
getting needed materials

## Bibliography

Reardon, J. 1993. "Developing a Community of Scientists." In *Science Workshop: A Whole Language Approach*, ed. W. Saul et al. Portsmouth, NH: Heinemann.

*Consumer Reports*. Yonkers, NY: Publication of Consumers Union of U.S.

*Zillions: Consumer Reports for Kids*. Yonkers, NY: Publication of Consumers Union of U.S.

# 11 Mary Beth Johnson

# Looking for Hope in All the Wrong Places

*"Leaves are important in the forest. A lot of animals and insects live under them."*

*"Brookside Nature Center made a place for animals to live."*

*"We don't know who used to live there or who used to cook there."*

"Oh, no," I groaned as I read my fourth graders' science "research." Their writing was disastrous—and especially so after all the time they had invested in their research. Panicked, I called the nearest writing expert available to me, Dr. Wendy Saul. Wendy, an author of science books, is known for her interest in children's science writing. As project director for the Elementary Science Integration Project (ESIP), she has helped many classroom teachers with student projects. We arranged a time to meet to discuss the "problem." Without seeing the writing, Wendy asked for a history of my project. . . .

Hello. Welcome to the Brookside Nature Trail. You will see ten stations while on this trail. At this first station, you can see three levels—the canopy, which is the top level; the understory, which is the middle level; and the ground level, is almost the bottom level. The underground is the fourth level which you can't see.

Extracts throughout this chapter are the children's final submissions for the nature guide. These were later edited by Brookside Nature Center staff and made available to visitors in a printed brochure.

It had all begun innocently in October, when my principal approached me, asking if I was interested in working on a science project with a naturalist from a nearby nature center. My interest piqued, I met with Sara Lustbader from the Brookside Nature Center, and learned that she wanted to work with one teacher and a class on writing a guide for ten stations on a walking trail. Sara had helped set up a similar project in Arizona; however, she had moved before it was completed. Because of my commitment to integrating science and writing, this seemed to be the perfect project for me. I was filled with excitement as Sara and I drew up a time line of our goals. Because the nature center was within walking distance, we planned visits almost every month throughout the school year. On our timeline, May seemed a long way away. We also decided to divide the class into ten groups of three, with each group responsible for researching and writing the text for a particular station on the trail. In addition, each group would also create artwork and writing that reflected the character of the station.

> Station Two is the disturbed area. This area has one part that is old and one part that is new. If you come back in twenty years, the area with brush will be made up of small trees.

I was thrilled, but overwhelmed. How would I figure out who could work together? Who would be able to research such diverse topics? Where would I find the research materials? Would my students be able to read and understand the books if I could get them? Even if we had the materials and they could read them, could they write about the information they discovered?

And how would I incorporate the heterogeneity of my class? Children from Bolivia, Vietnam, Korea, and China were still going to ESL classes to learn English. Two other students were being mainstreamed even though they had major learning disabilities. I had eight children reading below grade level as well as six reading above. How would these kids work together to complete all the research and write up their findings? I started to have a sinking feeling.

> Welcome to Station Three, also known as the creekside. Tadpoles and waterstriders live in the creek in the warmer months. In winter, the creek is not frozen, but still running. In the fall, the trees—sycamores and willows—shed their leaves. The leaves float away and can end up in the Chesapeake Bay.

As a class we embarked on our first walking field trip. The weather was cool and sunny, and the Brookside Gardens near the Nature Center were a beautiful sight of red and gold leaves. Everyone met the staff of the Nature Center and then tramped along the pathways to their respective stations. It was a perfect beginning. When we returned to the classroom, each student wrote about the three stations they thought were most interesting and gave reasons why they would want to research that area or topic. As I read each piece, I tried to think of who should work together, who possessed reading and research skills, and who were our artists. Finally, I divided up the class into ten teams and assigned each a station.

The next day we began our research in earnest. Now that the stations were real to the students, they dove into the books I had brought in from both the school and the public library. Although some teams used reams of paper to write about every creature or plant found in the meadow or creek, other teams cried out in frustration. "Mrs. Johnson, there's nothing in this book about succession, or decaying logs, or Maryland cabins." The research ground to a halt in some cases when teams gave up. The Native American team was researching the Zuni tribes, not the Eastern Woodland Indians. Everyone was working hard, but it seemed impossible to keep tabs on the direction they were going. I began meeting with individual teams at recess and going over their research. This helped calm some of the chaos.

> Station Four: Double and Triple Trees. When a live tree gets cut down, the roots do not die. The stump will soon grow several new branches from all the energy stored in the roots. Many winters will pass and the new branches will grow into trunks. Why do you think some of these trees were cut down?

After the next visit, winter weather and holiday schedules severely curtailed our planned visits to Brookside. Sara, accompanied by other naturalist staff members, came to our classroom and answered the students' questions. They brought live animals from the nature center, such as rat snakes and box turtles. The children were thrilled to be able to touch the cool dry snakeskin and the hard shells. The naturalists also brought stuffed owls and squirrels for the students to examine closely. The children always had questions, and these visits in the dead of winter sparked new research possibilities. When we encountered a lot of difficulty with some of the topics, such as succession and Eastern Woodland Indians, Sara pulled materials from the public library and the center's library that were even more specific to the research. I watched as the students began writing poems that described their stations. Other team members worked on illustrations to accompany their text, and some even tried to create short activities that could be done at the station.

> Welcome to Station Five. This stop is about a decaying log. It has been decaying for a long time and is a part of a cycle. First, it was a healthy young tree. After it grew, it became old, fell down and began to decay. Finally it decayed completely and turned into soil.

As Sara and I began to go over the folders for each station, we realized that for the most part, the text was disjointed and seemed only to be a conglomeration of interesting facts. Although the students had gleaned a great deal of information from their research, they seemed reluctant to "let go" of these facts. Despair began to set in. We had worked hard—why didn't the writing reflect this? How could I show Sara and the naturalists that the kids really did have good ideas? How could I help the students "fix" their writing without doing it for them?

Enter Wendy, who, after hearing all of this, pronounced, "They're not ready to write yet." What? Not ready? If they don't get ready soon, the naturalists may rewrite the whole thing themselves. How could they even suggest such a thing, after all the time we've put into the project? What could I do to help my students?

At Wendy's suggestion, we gathered brochures from local parks, and, as a class, brainstormed the plusses and minuses of each. Then we looked at some of our writing to see if it contained these positives and negatives. In the same way we visited the stations, making analyses of each area and deciding what science topic was important to research and write about, we analyzed our writing and that of others to help us make decisions about what to edit.

Because the students' activities at the end of the text seemed too rigid and closed-ended, Wendy suggested that the naturalists come to class to participate in small group, open-ended activities, such as passing around a turtle shell or snake skin and having each student say something they knew about it. We tried this and a closed-ended activity, where we had to identify a tree by its leaf, with teams competing to match the correct leaf. When the naturalists left, as a class we talked about which activity we liked and why. We first discussed how we felt when we were "winning" or "losing", or just sharing. We tried to explore the way our reading audience would feel when they tried an activity in our brochure. Then the students wrote why either a closed- or open-ended activity would help their station.

> Station Six: Native Americans lived in this area thousands of years ago. There were many tribes in Maryland that could have lived here but the Potomacs probably lived in this area. Native Americans cared for the earth and nature. They used things in the forest in their daily lives.

Finally, after many rewrites and team conferences, it was time to write again. By this point in the year, my students were becoming comfortable with the new Macintosh computer lab. In fact, we were one of the first classes to initialize our own disks and use the writing center for our poetry unit. I realized that each team should put its information on the disks, since rewrites were a matter of a few quick changes by keystroke instead of the time-consuming and laborious hand-copying of pages. Moreover, spellcheck could help highlight small errors. The naturalists could thus spend their time focusing on the writing itself instead of the aesthetics. Why hadn't I thought of this before?

> You are at Station Seven, the quiet spot. It is time to rest.
> Look back at the hill you just walked up. Relax. Enjoy our quiet spot poem.

It was spring. The trees were beginning to bud. Temperatures were rising. We could finally go back to Brookside and compare our observations of the stations from early fall and winter. Final drafts were ready to show to the center staff. Parents, canceled from earlier trips, were mobilized to accompany us. What we didn't count on was the Blizzard of '93, which kept us from school for four days. Luckily the naturalists came through and together we met with each team to go over the writing. This time, I sat in to take notes on each and every meeting. Teams that were not conferencing with the naturalists were busy working on illustrations or creative writing pieces for their stations. What I had found before was that teams developed amnesia when asked to remember specific suggestions as to how to clarify their topic. The other problem was that one naturalist would suggest an approach that the kids would pursue and then another naturalist would tell them to ignore it. Because of this, I became an adult voice with a memory and notes. This time, the naturalists were surprised at the depth and clarity of the students' writing, and were amazed at the improvement. I was ecstatic and my kids were proud.

> Station Eight: The meadow is a natural habitat. If we were to lift up a small section of the grass and look underneath, we would see a natural highway for many of the animals that have their homes in the meadow.

What was the next step? I tried to think in writing terms and decided that we needed to test our writing on an audience. Luckily, the fourth-grade class had just enough fourth graders who could accompany us to Brookside Nature Center. We planned to take our writing there in order to let the other fourth graders view the site and hear our teams read what they wrote. The object was to see if what was seen and what was written matched. I explained to my class that often publishers have a review copy that people critique, and that week, I got a review copy in the mail. It was an omen. Things were going too smoothly.

> Station Nine: Welcome to the wildlife area. Don't just walk by. We want you to sit down and observe the wildlife. Many special plants have been planted here to attract animals and birds.

A beautiful, warm April day dawned. Was I really taking 44 fourth graders into the woods? Was I crazy? What would the other kids do? Would they distract my kids, or just be bored? In spite of my worries, the day went well. We had decided to videotape each station and celebrate by having a picnic before going to the stations; however, the person who was supposed to do the videotaping was sick, and I had only three parents and one teacher to spread over the ten stations while I videotaped. The naturalists were generous enough to give us three staff members to help us, and the taping went well. The kids were really excited about the project, and the staff was just as impressed by the final product.

Station Ten: This cabin represents old pioneers who lived in this area around 200 years ago. People made cabins using wood, wood chips, and clay. The pioneers kept their food fresh by building a smokehouse near the cabin.

After editing the students' work, the staff turned the project over to the typesetter and printer, leaving me to ponder the lessons learned that year. Writing involves a lot of patience, and though at times I had encountered grave doubts about the feasibility of such a project, I learned that my belief and trust in my students was well founded. The students learned writing and research skills that they will be able to use in other areas. I believe we *all* learned that each class member could make a valuable contribution. Most important of all, I learned that there was, indeed, "a time to write." Finally, I asked my students to write about the whole experience—particularly the end. One wrote:

The flowers bloomed, buds are sprouting on trees, and the grass is as green as ever. On summer vacation, I'm going to go to Brookside. I'll visit all ten stations and think of my class and you.

## Appendix

This appendix lists some of the steps we took in working on this project. In addition, we have included some of the arrangements that helped the project flow more smoothly.

## Project Time Line

Develop a time line with possible dates for:

field trips
projected completion dates for rough drafts
illustrations
creative writing pieces
final publishing deadlines

Sketch out the responsibilities of each adult in the project in regard to field trips, writing, resources, and publication.

## Teams

After an initial field trip, divide the class into small teams according to:

- student interest
- student interactions
- student strengths (e.g., art, research, writing)

## Team Captains

Designate a team captain who will be responsible for getting materials, returning materials, and reporting any team problems. I chose able students who worked well with others, and privately encouraged them to help their teammates.

## Student Work and Folders

Set up an area where each team can store:

- all student work in a pocket folder
- specific books and resources
- team computer disk for word processing

This ensures that no work is lost or left at home. Plus, having all work in a folder helps the students get to work quickly. Having the team disk in the folder pocket cuts down on passing out and collection time, and means that research can be easily transported to the computer lab.

## Work Areas

Designate specific, permanent areas of the room for each team to work. This ensures that students don't waste time looking for a work area, and allows you to easily locate each team.

## Teacher's Notes

These ranged from notes on team conferences, such as what they were working on, what problems they encountered, what questions they asked, and what the status of their writing was. I stored these in a loose-leaf notebook with Team 1, Team 2, etc., at the top of each page. I also kept notes of the naturalists' suggestions on these team sheets when I found that conflicting ideas were given to the students, or the students "forgot" what the naturalists said.

## Scheduling Work Time

Originally, I would assign the entire class to work at the same time on their research, and I would then rotate from team to team observing and talking to students. Having only the captain report specific problems of working together or research problems cut down on a great deal of wasted time. As the project progressed, I found that I had to have working lunches to meet with individual teams in order to assess how far they had come and see what resources they still needed. Toward the end of the project, when several teams had completed their work, conferencing with individual teams while the whole class was supposed to be working was not as constructive.

## Brochures

Many groups are willing to send brochures, but you need to allow enough time to receive them. We requested brochures by phone from local parks and trails, but it took a while to get several different types.

## Editing and Final Publication

Allow time for editing and reworking drafts. We had to rework the artwork for the final publication because the illustration size no longer fit with the typesetting and spacing of the final draft.

# 12 Twig C. George

# Writing Eco-Mysteries

"Writing ecological mysteries," explains author Jean Craighead George to a group of students clustered around her, "is really writing a scientific investigation. It's a translation of the scientific process into a form of literature called a mystery. Who likes a good mystery?" Every hand goes up, some fingers clutching pens, some the magnifying glass they were asked to bring with them. "The only difference," she continues, "is that instead of a murderer or villain you have an ecological problem." The children nod and some make notes in their handmade journals. Today, twenty kids between the ages of eight and twelve will be detectives at Teatown Lake Reservation in Croton-on Hudson, New York. They have gotten up early to attend a workshop led by Jean and the nature center biologist, Rod Christie. They will investigate the area and write their own ecological mysteries in the genre that Jean developed during her productive career as a children's book author of nearly seventy science literature books.

One of the children in the group is Jean's granddaughter, Katie. Like the other children, it is her job today to find a mystery and solve it with the information she learns from Rod and her grandmother, who will lead them through the woodland.

"We got to hear about things from Grammy and Rod," Katie remembers. "I liked it because we walked around and wrote down what we thought. I wrote down everything I heard and saw and smelled." The details noted carefully in the children's ever present journals may become part of the setting and narrative of their mysteries, or they may turn up in something else they write months later. In her journal, Katie writes:

| I hear | I smell | I see |
|---|---|---|
| pepers | skunk cabbage | crows |
| ducks | raccoon | bugs |
| people | dead bugs | fireflies |
| birds | wood peckers holes | geese |
| cars | fungus | |
| wind | | |
| crunching leaves | | |
| scraping sticks | | |
| me scratching my pen | | |

"We gave them a scenario," Rod recalls. "It went something like this: An environmental consultant was hired by the board of directors to make the reserve better for hiking, boating, swimming. Better for people. Then we described several events that could have occurred around the nature center which would have broader ecological effects—dredging the pond, getting rid of the marshy areas, making the vernal ponds deeper, removing dead trees that might fall on someone, and mowing the fields for Frisbee™-playing and picnics."

Jean, Rod, and the students discussed the consequences of these actions as they toured the site. "We just didn't try to figure out *a* mystery," Katie explains. "We saw things and solved other mysteries, too. I saw stuff I didn't know. I saw salamanders under dead trees—and in the stream. That's how I figured out it wasn't good to take all the dead trees or dredge the pond."

One of the interesting results of approaching science through eco-mysteries is that the children make connections naturally and enthusiastically that they would not necessarily make on just a "nature walk." For example, Katie writes:

**Shoudens**
They shouden cutdown the trees because the animals live there.
They shoudent make the pounds deeper because the fish will come a the
    salamander will go.
They shoudent moe the fields because the mice live there.

"They got it," Rod says. "They did real well and understood the concepts. Some of the ideas were tough, and it took awhile, but they thought it through themselves. We do so many programs for so many children and we have to constantly watch that we don't become entertainers or just try to find something new—that we really teach them something. Nature walks give kids information, but if they don't use it regularly, they don't retain it. The Eco-Mystery Project allowed the children the time and support to come to their own conclusions. Jean George's example as a writer, the goal of a mystery to solve, and the discipline of keeping the journals slowed the pace down and made the work meaningful. As a result, the project had that long-term continuity we look for."

The rest of the morning was spent looking at bird beaks, designing hypothetical birds (Katie points proudly to a bird in her journal that she designed to eat oatmeal), making maps of the nature center, and talking about possible mysteries and solutions. "We ran out of time," Katie admits. So Katie dictated the following story to her grandmother:

### The Case of the Missing Field Mouse

*by Katie Pittenger*

The owner of Teatown Lake Reservation, Rod, called up Stacy Haynesworth, nature detective.

"All the field mice are gone, and could you find out why?" he said.

"Well, have you done anything new with the reservation?" Stacy asked.

"Yes, we have," he said.

"I'll be right over."

At 12:15 P.M. Stacy came with her notepad, her pen, and her magnifying glass. Rod showed her where the field mice were missing. They walked through lush, beautiful woods. All the underbrush had been neatly trimmed, and there were bugs crawling all over their legs because they cut down the dead trees.

When they got to the vernal pond that should dry up in summer, she saw that there were no salamanders or mosquitoes because the board of directors had dredged the pond and turned it into a deep swimming hole.

"Those fish in there eat the salamanders," said Stacy, "but that doesn't affect the mice."

After a while they came to the Teatown Lake. It had been

dredged, too. There were only people swimming and boating. There were no weeds so there were no fish. But that didn't affect the field mice, either.

Then, after all that, they got to the field. It looked like a golf course. All the wildflowers had been mowed, and the grass was about two inches tall. Then Stacy knew why the mice had gone away.

"The villain," said Stacy, "is the mower."

"The mower!" said Rod. "What did the mower do?"

"The mower mowed all the wildflowers away and so there were no seeds for the mice and they went away. Also the hawks and owls could see them and catch them."

Rod told the board of directors to replant the wildflowers and put the tall grass back anyway they could.

In about half a year the field mice had come back.

The End

Katie and the other children shared their dictated stories, then asked for Jean's signature on their journals.

"I should be asking for yours," she told them, and the young authors obligingly signed her notebook.

When Jean published her first ecological mystery, *Who Really Killed Cock Robin?*, in 1971, she never dreamed that almost 25 years later children would be reading her book and the other ecological mysteries that followed, then walking out of their classrooms and writing their own mysteries by observing the natural events around them. But because of the Elementary Science Integration Project (ESIP), inspired teachers, and the natural curiosity of children, that is exactly what is happening.

## Eco-Mysteries as Teaching Tools

The idea of using Jean's ecological mystery series as a model for integrating language arts and science was the result of a project begun by English teacher Cheri Jefferson and her eighth-grade students at Patuxent Valley Middle School in Jessup, Maryland. After a summer spent exploring the possibilities of combining science, literature, and writing at ESIP, Cheri began to look for ways to infuse her eighth-grade English classes with science. A mitigated wetland on school property that was being created to replace a natural wetland that was destroyed nearby seemed like an interesting and natural focus for her project. But what would she *do*?

An award-winning English/language arts teacher, Cheri loves Shakespeare and words. She is pretty and prim and always wears clean sneakers. Though she had attended the month long ESIP summer workshop, she still did not consider herself a "science person." Nevertheless, she was confident enough as a teacher to organize a diverse group of students to explore the issue before her.

"I began simply by encouraging my students to 'read around' in the science literature of Jean Craighead George," Cheri explains. "I had the kids look at how, in Ms. George's books, the science and prose were intertwined so tightly that it is hard to separate one from the other. They also began keeping journals."

The students visited the wetland to observe wildlife, seasonal changes, colors, textures, and other details that interested them. In their journals they recorded their activities: testing water, identifying bugs, and keying out plants. Although the class was fun and the kids were enthusiastic, no real project had emerged.

As they continued to read and observe, they came across Jean's three ecological mysteries, *The Missing Gator of Gumbo Limbo, Who Really Killed Cock Robin?*, and *The Fire Bug Connection*. Then something clicked: One group asked if they could write their own wetland mysteries. And not just stories but books, with chapters.

"I wasn't sure I could do this," Cheri confesses. "I knew the kids could write, but I was not sure that I was comfortable enough with the science to help them succeed with it." She knew the project had potential, so she turned to the expert, Jean George.

"Ms. George was very encouraging," Cheri recalls. "She wrote a letter to the class and told them how she went about writing eco-mysteries herself."

Dear Eco-Mystery Writers:

When I began writing eco-mysteries it was considered a new genre of literature. I am very excited to hear that now you will be contributing your own work to this field. This is how I think of them.

Ecological mysteries are an investigation into nature. They can be as straightforward as "Why is the sky blue?" to more complicated mysteries such as "Who killed the trout?", or "Where have the turtles gone?" So, in the process of writing your mystery you pursue your own line of questioning which, in turn, becomes the basis for your story.

Ecological mysteries are solved by following "scientific methods." Let me take you through the steps I use to write an ecological mystery.

1. Identifying the problem (the mystery)
The trout are dead, the turtles are missing.
2. Solving the problem
   a. Careful observation and research
   b. Experiments
   c. Citing regularities, such as the air is clean, the water temperature is normal. This helps you see what is regular.
3. Explanations and conclusions
You solve the mystery. Can you find the connections between the "problem" and what you have learned from your research and observations?

The ecological mystery writer embellishes the scientific method with protagonists, place, time, scenery, plot, suspense, and poetic writing, and has a good time putting it all down. Unlike scientists, you might know the answer before you begin your story, but as a good mystery writer you save it until the end.

## Pre-investigation

I read *Science News*, *Science*, *Natural History*, and many other journals whose writers have identified a mystery and are trying to solve it, for instance, why are the frogs disappearing?

### 1. Identifying the Problem (The Mystery)
You need to know the problem (your mystery) before you begin, but you may not know all the answers. I knew "who done it" in *The Fire Bug Connection* before I started writing, because of an article I read in *Scientific American*. The villain was a balsam fir tree. How's that for a murderer!

In *Who Really Killed Cock Robin?*, I did not know the villain and I did my research as I wrote. I had wanted the robin in *Who Really Killed Cock Robin?* to have a final deadly killer—like the arrow, as in the poem, *Who Killed Cock Robin*: Who killed cock robin? "I," said the sparrow, "I killed cock robin with my little arrow." "The arrow," I said to myself, "is going to be the murderer." But what is it? I went to scientific journals and listened to scientists to find out.

Inadvertently, I found that arrow. I happened to read in a Florida paper that seeds preserved in fungicide were sowed in a field. They were eaten by blackbirds. The birds died immediately. The tiny insects that live under the birds' feathers left their former hosts and jumped onto a flock of migrating robins that came down to the field for worms. The insects bit and took enough blood from the robins to weaken them. That, I said, is the fatal arrow. Cock Robin, already worn down by the many pollutants in his environment, could not survive the insect bites. They were the straw that broke the camel's back. Cock Robin died.

## 2. Solving the Problem (The Mystery)

a. Careful observation

I always visit the area where I set my story. I take notes on the animals and plants in a journal. I write down the sights, sounds, and smells—anything that will help me remember how it feels to be there. I go back to these notes when I write my mystery.

I also note possible clues. For instance, again in *Who Really Killed Cock Robin?*, I visited a town where a cotton mill used toxic chemicals. Farmers beyond the town sprayed pesticides, and people used herbicides on their lawns. I worked all these observations into my story.

b. Experiments

Experiments are a good way to solve your mystery. I try to do my own experiments. I test water, air, measure rain, and once asked a biologist to test the tissues of a baby robin that had died in my yard. Why did it die? Chemical poisoning. Now I had a victim and a criminal. The next question is, Where did the chemical come from?

There are many experiments you can do at school to solve your mystery. Go find an insect net, a magnifying glass, a water testing kit, make a rain gauge, or even set up a bird-feeding station. Take notes in your journal on your discoveries.

c. Citing regularities

Like a scientist, I "cite regularities." There is enough rain? That is not it. It has not been extremely hot or cold. So that cannot be it. There is a good food supply. Starvation is out. But there has been a significant habitat disturbance—a development has cut trees, bulldozed the ground, muddied the stream. Here, then, is an irregularity and a possible villain.

## 3. Explanations and Conclusions (Solving the Mystery)

Suppose your mystery is why the trout have vanished from a stream. You have tested the water, noted possible pollution sources, checked the river for regularities: the temperature was correct, there was enough food, and there are not too many predators. You've talked to the experts. Now it is time to put it all together. What's going on? What has happened to the trout? You've got it? Great.

Now you have a story. In writing it, take your readers with you through everything you did or researched.

## 4. Writing Your Mystery

a. Characters

Create your nature detective. He or she should be a child (if you are writing for children) who has reason to care about your mystery problem. Does he/she live in the area you are writing about? That is usually best. Perhaps he/she can't find a wild animal that has always been there.

He/she might notice a change, such as too many weeds in a stream, or no frogs in the spring. Supporting characters can be sources of information. A conservation officer can tell your detective about the laws; a farmer enlightens him about fertilizers and fungicides; a neighborhood naturalist knows what the plants and animals are; and a fisherman knows the stream. There are many possibilities.

Give background on your nature detective. Briefly describe him or her, how he/she became involved in the problem, and where he/she lives, parents, etc. Feed this information to the reader as the story progresses.

b. Audience

It is important to know for whom you are writing your mystery. Is it children your age? You might want to write your mysteries for the students in another grade in your school, for instance. If you know your audience, your mystery is a lot easier to write.

c. Red Herrings

Don't forget, a good mystery writer leads the reader down a few dead ends before revealing the final solution. Be sure to add a few "wrong turns" to your story to keep your readers guessing.

## A Sample Story Line

Your detective's name is Chris (I am going to make her a girl this time).

The trout have died in a woodland stream. Chris first suspects the water. She gets a water testing kit from the school science lab. On the back of the testing kit it says there are eleven possibilities for pollution that might kill fish. The presence of two or three of these, or even one in some cases, might end the mystery, but Chris finds the water is clean. Now what?

She sees a misty cloud and suspects the air. Chris calls the weather bureau and asks for the air pollution index in her area. Is there acid rain? If there is acid rain, that might end the story. The air is clean. On to some people research.

Chris meets a fisherman and suspects him. But after talking to him she learns that a great blue heron has been eating all the fish in a pond near his house.

Chris suspects the great blue herons. She sets up a blind, or a video camera, to observe her stream. Or, she could read a book and learn that herons fish in ponds and marshes, but not in fast, running, woodland streams. She concludes it is not the heron.

Next, Chris notices the dead weeds. She calls the State Fish and Game department and finds that plants take oxygen out of the water when they decay. Chris tests the water. There is not enough oxygen in the water for trout! But why did the weeds die? She checks around her neighborhood and learns that the golf course uses weed killers. She tracks the water from the golf course sprinklers with a colored dye that turns up in the stream. The water is carrying the weed killer into the stream. Here is the real culprit.

Chris asks the owner of the golf course to stop using weed killer. He cooperates. Then she asks her friends to help her remove the dead weeds. The trout come back. The case is solved.

I hope this will help you write your own ecological mystery, and examine nature in a new and exciting way.

Good Luck! JCG

Cheri's class continued their investigation of the streams and marshes. Because she was not a "science person," Cheri let her students do the work of finding the answers to their scientific mysteries. As a result, they went far beyond what might have been covered in an information-oriented class. Like the children at Teatown Lake, they were motivated. They interviewed naturalists, called state and federal offices for information, and read and read. They were also required to conduct experiments and make observations at the site that would support their ideas. They inventoried insects and "read" tracks to discover what other animals and birds depended on the wetland.

As they became more involved in their projects, they decided, with encouragement from all involved, to invite Jean to visit the class in April, an invitation to which she accepted happily. The result was a day of activity, exploration, musing, and videotaping! Armed with nets, collecting tanks, and journals, Jean and the class explored the wetland and continued down into the river. They tested water for oxygen, nitrates, and pH levels. When the day was over it was quite clear that Cheri Jefferson's sneakers would never be the same again and neither would her classes.

## Success "Stories"

Since that day in April 1993 many ESIP teachers, naturalists, and even Jean have led eco-mystery projects. For children and young people who really like fiction, eco-mysteries provide a great way to get into science. Elementary teachers who see their students all day find themselves with even more opportunities to integrate science into other parts of the curriculum. A student in Patti Winch's fourth- and fifth-grade class composed the following for a class assignment:

### Who Really Killed the Box Turtle?

*by Jason Primrose*

### Chapter I: The Box Turtle

It was a dewy morning and Joanne and I were walking to Hollin Meadows Elementary.

My name is Jessica and I am eleven years old. My friend's name is Joanne. She is 4′2″, she is light brown with silky brown-reddish hair, and she is also eleven.

I am 4′4″, I am brown too, except darker than Joanne. My hair is a dark black and it's silky too.

We meet each other at the corner of Hybla Valley Avenue and go to the field in the back of the school. We try to go early so we won't be late for school. When we get there, I see my box turtle, Akismarioh, coming toward us. We go to him. Then the bell rings and we rush in to meet our teacher.

### Chapter II: Dead

"Hello girls," Mrs. Wayder said.

"Hi, Mrs. Wayder," we say together.

We sit at our seats. Brooom putt putt putt putt. Oh no! I look outside, whew, just the lawn mower.

I must have been going mad or it really happened. Something got sliced up under the lawn mower and I thought it was Akismarioh. Then after that I said that my imagination must be going wild. It could have been anything.

As Joanne and I were walking at recess, she saw that the swings were open, and told me she would be back. I have an ex-friend named Lisa who came and talked to me.

"Hi," she says in a fake, sweet voice.

"Hi," I say rolling my eyes in a nasty way. After all, she did steal my mother's ring last year.

I see her turn away and leave. After a few minutes Joanne is back. I smile and say, "Let's go see Akismarioh and Dragon, my garter snake."

I go over near Akismarioh and see clearly that he and Dragon are dead. Then I whispered, "The lawn mower, the lawn mower. I'll get the lawn mower."

## Chapter III: It's Alive

It turns out my garter snake is alive. The reason I thought Dragon was dead was because he was lying on his back and it looked like he wasn't breathing. I'm still furious with the lawn mower for killing Akismarioh.

I go over to Dragon. The long, thin, twisted tree vines hang from a bent, half dead tree. This dead tree is where Dragon lives. Most of the things he eats live in there too.

School ended and like always I rushed into my house. "Hi, Mom," I say, starting immediately on my homework. She was drying dishes.

"Hello, Jessie," she says back. "What's the rush?" she asks, still wiping.

"I'm going to the field with Joanne after I finish my homework."

"No, you're not," she says giggling a bit. "You have your dentist appointment, remember."

"Darn," I whisper. I thought it would slip by her.

I'm getting braces today. I will look rotten in them, I know it. We wait for hours at the orthodontist. At least two.

Then finally I'm called. After one more hour I've got my braces and I'm out. It took us a half hour to get home, so when I met Joanne it was 4:10.

"What took you so long?" she asks frustratedly.

"My braces," I say back.

"Oh, I forgot," she says quietly.

We go to the yellow, white and pink honeysuckles. Dragon lies near the pearl bush. I call it that because it has only white honeysuckles.

At first I couldn't see him because he was green but after a while I could make out his eyes.

I thought the lawn mower did it, I really did. But I would soon find out who really killed the box turtle.

## Chapter IV: Describing the Forest Area

The next day I found my box turtle lying in the ruffled holly bushes. When I first saw him he was in the middle of the field—someone must have moved him since then.

Near these holly bushes there was bamboo. The bamboo had whitish powder on the outside of it, then a white substance under a thick covering of green. The dirt was splashed over the ground and was covered by bits and pieces of moss. Dragon was curled comfortably around a bamboo stick.

I saw Lisa near it, with a hammer! It looked like she was going to hit Dragon.

"Lisa," I scream, "Stop!"

Joanne runs up right behind me. "Yeah, stop it!" she yells.

"I wasn't doing anything, really," Lisa whines.

"What were you doing with a—plastic hammer?" I ask.

"Yeah," she says. "He chews on it."

"Sure," Joanne murmurs.

Lisa runs away. I walk closer to see he is no longer on the bamboo, he is on the ground with two hammer marks in his skin.

## Chapter V: Too Many Questions

Who's done it?

Was it Lisa?

Why did he or she do it?

Were they jealous or did they just want to see the joy of something dying? These thoughts swirled in my mind until school was over. I went to the field and saw the box turtle. (I don't call him by his name because he's dead.)

It had moved over near the poison ivy bushes and the poison oak. Fins and the head were stuck out of his shell, the shell was cracked open, with bits and pieces of shell lying next to it. Flies were drinking the blood and maggots were eating the liver. "Eeww," I mutter.

"Hi, Jessie," Joanne calls.

"Hi," I say.

"Look!" she exclaims. "A little hammer, like the one Lisa had."

"That's it! We've solved it," I cry.

"Huh?" she says, puzzled.

"The hammer she had yesterday, it's by Akismarioh's body!" I shout.

"Where is the connection?" she asks.

"Listen, a lawn mower blade spins, right?"

"Right," she says.

"Well, if a blade cut him up the pieces of shell would fly everywhere, and she must have cracked the shell because the shell pieces are close together and not spread out!"

"Now all we need is evidence," she says.

"Let's get the hammer," I exclaim.

"Wait! We can't forget fingerprints," she explains. "You get a pen. I'll get the tape. We need the fingerprints."

"Oh yeah," I add. "Get some gloves too. I've got a great way of getting her back."

"OK," she says. "I really can't believe she would do that, but don't worry, we'll get her back good."

## Chapter VI: Confronting Our Suspect

Today Joanne and I confronted the suspect, and that includes fingerprinting. We took tape, put it on the hammer, and got the fingerprint. We matched it up with Lisa's fingerprint—it matches!!—but we needed more evidence.

"You are dismissed," I say gleefully to Lisa.

"Jessica, why don't you have poison ivy?"

"What do you mean?"

"Jessica, you don't have poison ivy, and you stuck your arm all the way in it."

"They must have been fake leaves," I whisper, turning toward the window. "Either that, or it was regular ivy."

"Tomorrow let's confront our culprit," she shouts.

## Chapter VII: We've Got You

Today we saw Lisa, and she felt uneasy about us being there. I could see it in her eyes.

"Um, it's a pity how your turtle died," she says, smirking a bit.

Joanne was ready to stuff her like an animal. I pushed her back.

"Stop, Joanne. Don't let her know you're mad."

After that Joanne straightened up a bit.

"We know you did it," I say. "Your fingerprints match the

ones on the hammer. Your hammer was sitting by my turtle."

"The pieces weren't scattered so the lawn mower didn't
do it. You did."

"You also killed my garter snake."

"How did you find out?" Lisa screams.

"Just now," I burst out laughing, "and from the evidence," I say, pulling myself together.

"Shoot! I thought I was slick," she whispers angrily.

"Gets 'em every time," I giggle, nudging Joanne.

"Oh yeah, sister. You everything but slick." We laugh
again.

She's caught, finally. Now I know who really killed
Akismarioh.

### Chapter VIII: Detention

For killing a school animal Lisa was put in detention for
two weeks. She got no recess. She wasn't allowed to leave the
office without an adult. She had to eat lunch there, go to the
bathroom in the office, and she also had to do her school
work there. Her mom had to pick her up each day. Also, she
had to take care of the office's fish so she would learn to appreciate animals.

I told her I'd get her back and I did. She was caught, pun-
ished, and taught a lesson. But my pets weren't back, they
were gone forever. Too bad she wasn't!

### Chapter IX: My New Box Turtle

I found another box turtle and I fed her like Akismarioh,
except I took this one home. I named her Chun Li. Stupid
name, I know, but I loved it.

I wonder how long I will keep this box turtle? Should I
let her roam free? Will Lisa kill this one? Will she get me back
again? If she kills Chun Li, I won't be able to get her as easily
as I did this time, or will I?

So many questions. Oh well, for right now Chun Li is
safe, and so am I.

## Exploring Resources

Kathy Shell, at the John Ruhrah School in Baltimore City, began by reading
*The Missing Gator of Gumbo Limbo* with her students. She soon had a yel-

low legal pad, each line filled with issues her children were interested in re-searching. These issues ranged from the migration of the Northern Oriole to the levels of aluminum in the water supply. She did not know all the answers or even have reference sources for all of the questions that were emerging. She turned to another faculty member, ESIP teacher Carolyn Smith. "Kathy and I embarked on an adventure neither of us will forget," Carolyn recalls. "While Kathy's class was exploring eco-mysteries, I started an afternoon Science Discovery Club. Kathy and I developed strategies to assist children with finding the answers to their questions. They divided into writing groups and everyone shared the answers they discovered. The phone was used to call Enoch Pratt Library and the National Aquarium in Baltimore. Books were ordered from poison control. There was so much traffic in the office that the principal agreed to hook up a modem in the classroom."

Not all of the questions were answered. Some of the issues were geared toward research, some lent themselves to hands-on experiments, and some to local observations. Others were soon left behind. "The children in the Science Discovery Club used experiments to solve their ecological mysteries," Carolyn explains. "Then we took a field trip to Bragg Nature Center in January. The trails were frozen, the pond was a skating rink, but we had a wonderful naturalist who showed us that what appeared dead was just preparing for new growth in the spring." She stops and smiles. "That trip really brought the 'Ahhh' back to their writing. For me this project really explored the challenges of bringing ecological experiences to a city classroom. I learned that children only need a spark to embark on a journey to discover ecological issues. Using the resources within your own city and state is all you need to begin the journey."

Sharon Delgado, a teacher now at Jacksonville Elementary School in Baltimore County, developed a slightly different approach to research for her class. "First, we brainstormed a list of resources and experts the kids could contact. Then, as they needed information we would go in and call the expert. At first we would both try to listen on the same phone and take notes. Then—I think it was Anna—noticed that there was a speakerphone. That gave us the idea of recording conversations with experts for the whole class and making an archive." The kids then developed a list of experts for their mystery and composed a series of questions.

"We commandeered the conference room and a phone line for the entire day," Sharon recalls. "Anna stayed in the room and helped everyone with the tape machine and speakerphone—we called scientists, lawn service experts, and vets. They were all great. They loved the idea. We asked permission before we recorded them, of course." The tape archive was used as a resource by everyone in the class.

Access to a good supply of field guides, resource files of science current events, journals such as *Science, National Geographic, Scientific American*, an encyclopedia or one of the on-line computer networks, are also useful resources for helping the children find the information they need to solve their eco-mysteries.

Susan Wells' fifth-grade class at Carroll Manor Elementary School, also in Baltimore County, never got to the mystery writing. She began, as Cheri and the others did, reading Jean's books and analyzing the weaving of prose and science. She took the students outside once a week and had them begin journals.

"At first I was afraid they wouldn't have anything to write about," Susan says. "But when they know they will have to write, they are more focused. They had thirty minutes to write in their journals when we came inside. Many of them could have used more time." When her students first began the process of observing and journal keeping, Susan gave her class a focus. She asked them to make predictions, to pick something to observe over time, to use drawings, to identify what they were seeing. The following year Susan decided to introduce the project by building mini-ecosystems using *Bottle Biology* by Mrill Ingram. "Building the bottle biology columns made them observe more carefully when we were outside," recollects Susan. "They quickly noticed the relationships between things and how one's actions can affect everything else." As time went on, it was no longer necessary to provide a focus. They had built up a log of experiences to draw upon, and questions to return to: Why did the gold finches turn gold in spring? What happened to the animals when the snow and ice covered the ground? They recorded their thoughts in response journals.

Susan's first eco-mystery year turned out to include one of the worst winters in history. At times six inches of ice covered the ground. Still she continued to take the children outside to observe in the harshest weather, even if it was for only ten minutes. That ten minutes resulted in one of the most memorable walks of the year.

Later in the year Susan instructed her students to compare journal entries from two different days. "Since we started the project earlier in the year, when spring came they really noticed the changes," she remembers. Students wrote detailed observations, some in narrative and some in list form. One student's modified list appears below.

| 3/25/94 | Both | 4/22/94 |
|---|---|---|
| snow | grass | grass is |
| colder | trees |   darker |
| no leaves on trees | a little mud | flowers |
| couldn't see the sky | bit of water | trees have |
|   all clouds | things growing |   leaves |
| parts of tree falling |   from the tree | warmer |
|   off | both pretty | you could see |
| | |   the sky |
| | | onion grass |
| | | pretty and lite |

When the year ended, the mysteries had never been written, but the children's writing had become rich and exciting. For instance, Cara Bianchini compared a tree in Jean's *The Missing Gator of Gumbo Limbo* with a tree in her own school yard that she had been observing:

### Mine and Hers

hers is an oak so big and tall
mine is a willow so short and small
her limbs could cover a tennis court
mine couldn't cover three picnic tables
On her branches there are blankets of orchids
My branches are bare and exposed
hers has butterflies and lizards chasing insects
mine is lucky to have a winter bird perch on it
hers is a theater of horror, suspense, and rage
mine is a theater of dryness, coldness and age
ours are both living breathing things
ours are both a new generation
ours are both equal, bold and brazen

*Cara Bianchini*

## Eco-Mysteries Teach More than Science

There were other benefits from the ecological mystery project. Kathy Shell noted a great deal of increased recreational reading: one boy wanted to read every one of Jean's books; another girl requested books for her birthday for the first time. Another read over 8,000 pages for a "Rainforest Read-A-Thon," and raised over $100 with which the school bought five acres of rainforest.

Eco-mysteries teach writing skills as well as good science skills. Two of Kathy's students, Kimberly Black and Maria Mauroulis, entered their eco-mysteries in the writing contest for the local chapter of the International Reading Association and were the fourth- and fifth-grade winners. One student who had never liked writing wrote a seven-page eco-mystery. At the end of the year he applied and was accepted to the Summer Ingenuity Project at the middle school. On his application he wrote that he wanted to know more about pollution and ecology since he had become interested in them while doing research on his ecological mystery.

Sharon Delgado used the project to teach writing forms as well as science. "I start with a kernel of an idea," she says, "and then things begin to happen." One child wanted to write about nuclear explosions and aliens, another group couldn't come up with any ideas, and some elaborated too much and couldn't bring their ideas to closure. "So we read more, brainstormed the structure of a mystery, and used forms—I always make graphic organizers to help the kids learn to write in different styles. Once they have the structure, most become very creative with what they do with it. That's how we got into the epilogues. Two boys wrote a story about toxic waste. Along the way, they fell in love with their character," Sharon remembers with delight, "which is what you want to happen. They wanted to write more and more. So I suggested adding an epilogue that would bring you up to date on the character. In the end, a *lot* of them ended up writing epilogues, and all of them were different."

Since Cheri Jefferson began the project, eco-mysteries have taken many forms. Pearl Howell, at the Fairview Outdoor Educational Center in Washington County, Maryland, attended an ESIP eco-mystery workshop and started her fifth and sixth graders writing and producing eco-mystery puppet shows for the younger children at the center. The center now has more than forty puppets of native Maryland animals and a stage where the students can combine innovative uses of audio and visual technology while performing their mysteries.

Eco-mysteries can be done in a day at Teatown Lake, or over a year at Patuxent Valley Middle School. They can be done without ever leaving the classroom or without ever going into a classroom. However, something special seems to happen when the children go outside—for a minute, ten minutes, an hour, in every season and weather, all year long.

Even if your school is in the middle of a parking lot, there will be many things that are just waiting to be recognized: weeds that miraculously grow in the tiniest cracks of cement; puddles and drainage systems that eventually lead to waterways; and birds and butterflies that circle overhead.

By building bird feeders, planting butterfly gardens, providing brushy cover for rabbits, and leaving portions of dead trees for cavity nesters, woodpeckers, and other perching birds, you can bring wildlife to your school yard. As a result, you and your students will have more to observe, question, and write about. The Maryland Department of Natural Resources and the National Wildlife Federation both have free packets available to help you create habitats for wildlife in your school yard. It is conceivable that with minor modifications, millions of acres of public school property could contribute to the biological diversity of the countryside. Yet, even without any improvements, there still is much to see if you just get out and look.

Cheri, the original eco-mystery teacher, started her project with the idea that it would be finished by Christmas. But as the winter vacation drew closer, it became clear that the project was nowhere near completion. She had a dilemma: Should she quickly wrap up the project, or extend it? There was still a lot to do, and the students were excited about their work, so she decided that the project would be a full-year adventure. The group met once a week for fifty minutes over the course of an entire school year. In that time, they visited the wetlands every season, wrote in their journals, shared research, and had time to read and analyze the writing of Jean and other science literature writers. The time allowed the students to find answers, take in facts, watch the wetlands change from season to season, experience the different levels of activity surrounding the wetlands, and note the colors, smells, and moods of the marsh.

We often want children to learn quickly and efficiently so that we can move on to the next topic, unit, or book, and forget learning is neither neat nor efficient. Many things are understood over time through many sources. Whether you have a single day at Teatown Lake or a year to watch the wetlands, it is the long-term effects of the many forms of this project that make it intriguing. It is a project that should not be hurried. It should be savored. Good luck.

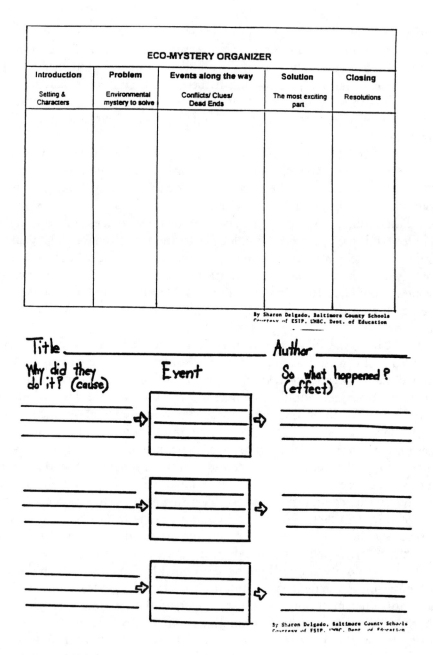

By Sharon Delgado, Baltimore County Schools
Courtesy of ESIP, UMBC, Dept. of Education

By Sharon Delgado, Baltimore County Schools
Courtesy of ESIP, UMBC, Dept. of Education

FIGURE 12–1

## Eco-Mystery Story Board

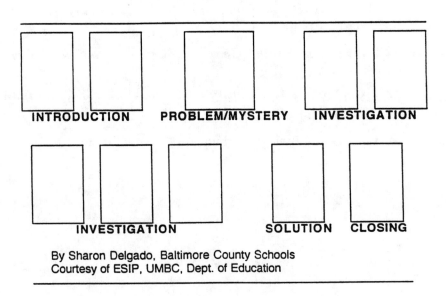

By Sharon Delgado, Baltimore County Schools
Courtesy of ESIP, UMBC, Dept. of Education

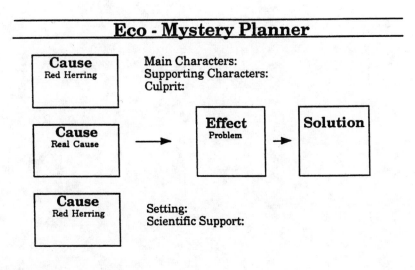

FIGURE 12–1 *(continued)*

## Bibliography

George, J.C. 1993. *The Fire Bug Connection: An Ecological Mystery*. New York: HarperCollins.

George, J.C. 1993. *The Missing Gator of Gumbo Limbo*. New York: HarperCollins.

George, J.C. 1971. *Who Really Killed Cock Robin?: An Ecological Mystery*. New York: HarperCollins.

Ingram, M. 1993. *Bottle Biology*. Dubuque, IA: Kendall-Hunt.

# 13 Barbara Bourne

# The Kids' Inquiry Conference: Not Just Another Science Fair

On May 27, 1993, at precisely 10:00 A.M., a big yellow school bus pulled up to a university campus. Twenty-seven fifth-grade students, carrying solar ovens, mealworms, terrariums, slides, photos, overheads, and posters, emerged from the bus and hurried across the parking lot. Within minutes they were joined by students from two other schools, also lugging boxes, bags, and jars filled with items they would need before the morning was over. A final check by teachers assured that everyone was ready—name tags were on, schedules in hand. Excitement was mounting . . . the First Annual Kids' Inquiry Conference© (KIC© '93) was about to begin.

By 10:30, three sets of slightly anxious yet remarkably poised fifth and sixth graders were standing in front of their student colleagues, sharing the highlights and results of the science research they had been conducting over the past several months. Later, they would sit as an audience, listening to the stories of other students' research. Then, they might join a small group tour of a working science lab or spend time in a "hands-on room," testing their wiles against the forces of erosion, tracking the paths of rivers, building structures that would withstand simulated earthquakes, or cracking open rocks, most of which contained genuine fossils.

Throughout the morning, children continued to take part in various sessions of sharing, listening, questioning, observing, and doing science. They conversed with student-scientists from distant communities; several even exchanged personalized, handmade business cards. Then, after mingling over an outdoor lunch, the participants joined in a discussion with noted children's science author Seymour Simon, gathered their conference Kid-KIC©-Packs, and headed for home, happy and excited about the day. They returned to their classrooms renewed and ready to continue their original science research, or anxious to explore something new.

The first chapter was written; the actualization of an idea was complete. The story that began with one teacher's desire to help students more effectively view themselves as scientists has since progressed to an annual forum in which hundreds of students from geographically and socioeconomically diverse schools come together each year to share, to listen, and to gain a new sense of themselves as learners, doers, and scientists.

## An Idea Evolves

What exactly is the Kids' Inquiry Conference? How was it conceived, and why do the teachers involved now feel it is such a vital part of their school year?

KIC© was conceived as a way for children to capture and share the excitement of scientific inquiry. Modeled after professional science conferences, it was designed to help students understand how adult scientists work and share information.

The idea was conceived by Charles Pearce, a fifth-grade teacher at Manchester Elementary School in rural Carroll County, Maryland. Charlie had long been searching out and implementing strategies that allowed for independent and authentic scientific investigation in his classroom (see Pearce 1993). After taking part in ESIP and growing as a teacher on his own, Charlie was witnessing increased levels of student inquiry and autonomy, a growing sense of community in the classroom, and mounting evidence of authentic science activity. With these changes, long-established methods of student reporting no longer seemed appropriate. The next point of change became clear.

My first year at ESIP, there was a great deal of discussion about authenticity—making connections across the curriculum and making learning in the classroom reflect, as much as possible, real life. We seemed to have several new notions converging. On the one hand, we were talking about inquiry in the classroom—how useful it was and what the kids were

gaining from it. At the same time, we were talking about authenticity—real ways for kids to share what they were discovering.

As I became more comfortable with inquiry, I felt that
the traditional means of sharing information—reports, magazine articles, even class presentations—weren't enough. I
wanted my students to go outside the classroom and share
what they were doing, the notions they were being struck by.
The idea of a conference where kids could share what they
were investigating seemed the perfect avenue for that.
(Pearce, interview.)

Charlie started discussing his idea of a kids' conference with other
teachers and members of the ESIP community. He felt the University of
Maryland Baltimore County (UMBC) campus where ESIP is held would
be an ideal setting, and the diversity of populations taught by other ESIP
teacher-led classes would further enrich his rural, mostly white student
body. But others were busy with their own new ideas. Charlie put the idea
on the back burner.

The idea remained little more than a distant vision until the summer of 1992. Veronica Stokes, a sixth-grade science teacher at Winston
Middle School, located in the heart of Baltimore City, attended a workshop led by Charlie at ESIP's second Summer Institute. When Veronica
heard Charlie's idea about students from different geographic and socioeconomic areas getting together to share what they were doing in science,
she was overjoyed. This was just what she'd been looking for!

Veronica was always searching out ways to spark an interest in
science in her students, African-American children who too often went to
school in old buildings equipped with run-down equipment and few supplies. She wanted to find ways for them to meet others interested in investigations similar to those she liked to set up in her classroom. And she
wanted her students to see themselves as valuable people, people who had
interesting and important scientific ideas, who could contribute to a
greater community of learners. With a kids' science conference, she hoped
she could help her students establish some common goals among themselves *and* with children from other schools. "Perhaps even break down
the race barrier a little," she explained. Furthermore, Veronica believed
that visiting a university campus would help her students set goals for their
future, whether or not those goals included a science career.

Finally, the kids' conference was moving from possibility to probability, but Charlie and Veronica felt that the project would be more successful if they could involve at least one other group of students. Before long, Susan Wells, a fifth-grade teacher at Carroll Manor Elementary School, located in a relatively affluent section of Baltimore County, decided to join in the process. With three teachers on board and the promise of help from ESIP staff, Charlie's dream was becoming a reality.

Details began to fall into place. The conference could be held at UMBC. There would be no university students on campus at the end of May, so the KIC© group could have complete access to the spacious commuter cafeteria. A "KIC© Committee," composed of the three teachers and several ESIP staff members, met periodically to set goals and plan a format and agenda for the big day. At the first planning meeting, the group chose a name and adopted Charlie's original conference goals.

The Kids' Inquiry Conference would provide students with opportunities to:

share the excitement of their own discoveries
interact with students from different schools who share common interests
view science as a dynamic force in their own lives
critically consider the credibility of their own research and the research of
    others
draw upon the discoveries of other students to enhance their own
    research

It was easy to find common ground around which they could plan. All three teachers wanted their students to interact with children from other ethnic, geographic, and socioeconomic groups. Many of the urban children had never left the city, and most of the rural and suburban children had little or no contact with children of different cultures and races. Still, all agreed that KIC© was not just an outlet for kids to meet other students.

> My students needed a place to go with what they'd been doing. I wanted them to take their discoveries to the outside world.
>
> And I didn't see this just for the children who had already made discoveries. I wanted a place where the others would say, "Hey, look. Kids like us can do investigations and find things out for themselves . . . and somebody cares. Maybe I can do that too." So I wanted a program not just for those who were already involved in inquiry, but a catalyst for those

who needed some encouragement to get involved. (Pearce, interview.)

Susan had a slightly different reason to become involved. She saw her involvement with KIC© as a way to ensure that *she* would value and promote more inquiry in the classroom. A young teacher with a specialty in reading, Susan felt that although she was finding more and more ways to get her students interested and involved in science, she was still on only the fringes of "inquiry."

It was soon evident that KIC© would be unlike anything these teachers (or their students) had ever encountered. It was definitely *not* just another science fair! There would be no elaborate displays of the "scientific method" fitting neatly onto three-paneled posters. Conference planners believed that KIC© presentations should take place as open-ended, student-to-student forums where young scientists would present their questions, their research to date, and the challenges they encountered while conducting their research. KIC© was to be a place for works-in-progress and would, therefore, require a whole new design.

While establishing the format of the conference, the committee referred frequently to what they knew about professional meetings and conferences. Because the primary focus of the day was to be students sharing the progress of their own investigations with others interested in similar ideas, "break-out" sessions would take up the bulk of the morning. At each session, two or three groups would present their research, grouped by common themes—consumer testing, technology, or perhaps mealworms and small creatures.

The committee wanted to take advantage of holding the conference at a science research university, so they set up tours of campus science labs. Charlie's class would design and staff a hands-on room where participants could "dig" into some new areas of science. Finally, the committee lined up keynote speakers. Dr. Freeman Hrabowski, UMBC president and math educator, would open the conference. The day would conclude with a talk by Seymour Simon, a favorite author of students from all three classes.

Plans were progressing and Charlie, Veronica, Susan, and their students were ready . . . or were they? Susan later admitted:

When I first heard about KIC©, I thought it was a great idea. But it became scary relying on my kids to do their own investigations and then formally presenting their findings to kids from other schools. Were they up to it? (Pearce, interview.)

Susan wasn't the only one nervous about allowing the children so much freedom. It was one thing to give the kids lots of latitude in the privacy of one's own classroom, but to bring them to a public forum, to invite them to develop their own reporting techniques, and expect them to conduct group discussions in front of their peers and celebrities like Seymour Simon—this was something else altogether. Even Charlie admitted to nursing a case of cold feet from time to time.

> As I got into this further and further, I had a certain amount of anxiety. I thought, "Wow! What have I gotten myself into? It may be a neat idea, but are my kids ready? Are they going to come through?" (Pearce, interview.)

Although these teachers had tremendous confidence in their students, they knew they had to do more than proceed on faith alone. Each in her/his own way had already established routines that supported inquiry, investigation, and student responsibility. Now KIC© was forcing them to expand on these routines and even establish new frameworks that would work in their individual classrooms.

## KIC© Moves to the Classroom

There were many elements common to the KIC© classrooms. In each classroom, students were encouraged to choose their own topics of investigation and develop testable questions. It did not matter if their investigations interested the teacher or any other students in the class, nor if there was a lot or only a little information in the library. And it did not matter if the area of interest did not fall under that year's curriculum, was a topic thought to be too difficult (or too simple) for children their age, or not quite "scientific" enough.

Despite the common ground, it must be noted (and indeed emphasized), that there was no one way to prepare for KIC©. ESIP encourages teachers to develop an instructional style that suits their own classroom needs and supports the curiosities and strengths of their students. Just as children are allowed to ask and research their own questions in their own ways, teachers must be free to pursue classroom inquiry in terms of their own goals, individual teaching styles, students' and school community needs, their schedule demands, and available resources.

Veronica worked in a departmentalized setting where she was assigned to teach only science, usually in forty-five-minute time blocks, and with specific content to cover and outcomes to meet. Within those confines she had to find time for the extended study and cross-curricular support necessary to promote the student-generated, open-ended questions suitable for KIC©. Charlie, on the other hand, was in a self-contained classroom, teaching the same children throughout most of the day. His students had been taught to develop testable questions directly from the science program, but were also encouraged to use literature, math, social studies, physical education, and daily activities as the basis for their science inquiry. So, as students began to think about their KIC© projects, it was only natural that their testable questions would spring from a variety of sources. Some questions, such as the those that led to two mealworm investigations, arose from the science "discovery boxes" (see Pearce 1993).

Other projects arose from less science-oriented sources. Based on the story line of *Hello, Mrs. Piggle-Wiggle* by Betty McDonald, two girls questioned whether grass would really grow when watered by tears. They knew that tears are salty and believed that salt water would inhibit, rather than encourage, grass to grow, so they conducted a controlled experiment to observe firsthand how salt water would affect plant growth. They planted six tiny plots of grass that they regularly watered from labeled jugs holding water of increasing salinity. Everyone was surprised to see that the grass watered from Jug B, the water with a small percentage of salt added, grew the most lush grass.

Charlie's students signed "contracts," agreeing to carry out their investigations and present their findings at KIC©. Presentation was voluntary, but all the children knew that signing and fulfilling the demands of a contract let them out of other, more mundane, classroom tasks. It was no surprise that many students jumped at the chance to prepare for and present at KIC©. The contracts were signed shortly before the students filled out a KIC© application and submitted it to the KIC© Committee.

Charlie developed the first KIC© applications that were quickly adopted, and of course adapted, by the other KIC© teachers. Similar to those required of adult scientists wishing to present their findings at professional conferences, applications to the KIC© committee were mandatory for all student presenters. These two-page questionnaires required basic information: name, school, grade, title and description of research project. The applications also asked for previous science research (e.g., school or scout projects, informal at-home investigations), and publications (e.g., reports, school newspaper articles). Applicants were delighted to have their earlier projects valued as important scientific work.

Application to present at the
**KIDS' INQUIRY CONFERENCE©**
KIC© '93

The Kids' Inquiry Conference Committee is eager to hear about your scientific research and discovery. In order to plan the conference, your assistance is needed.

Please complete the questions below as completely as possible.

Date   _January 3, 1995_

Name   _Lindsay Barron, Beth Hickey, Maureen Riley_
School   _7th District Elementary_   Grade _3_
Teacher   _Mrs. Galinski_

1. Describe any science-related reports or projects that you have prepared in the past two years.
*We did a project with food and we used Froot Loops, Soup, Muffins, etc. Some of us did a school newspaper. We did city projects, we made citys, and weather graphs about them and told about them.*

2. Have you published any science articles or stories in recent years (such as in a class or school newspaper or class journal)? If so, please list the topics of your publications.
*We made a school newspaper. And we made a book about the moon. We made dino adds about products that dinasaurs would need.*

3. List three discoveries you have made over the past two years (at school or elsewhere).
*We discovered that the moon change's diffrent shapes. We discovered facts about dinosaurs. We discovered about patterns. We discovered about citys. We also discovered about space and habitats. We discovered where the planets were, and pine trees, and about 3-D shapes.*

4. List the questions you are researching and would like to present at KIC© '95.

*What will happen when you roll two magnet marble's into each other? Can Magnets stick to anything beside metal. How many magnet's can stick together while holding them up in the air. How tall can you build Magnets?*

5. Describe your investigation at this point. What questions are you attempting to answer? How is your research progressing?

*We have planned what we are going to expirement and got the matireals. We are attempting to answer How high can you build magnets? Can magnets stick to anything besides metal? What will happen when you roll two magnet marbles into each other? How many things can stick to one magnet at one time? Why do magnets stick together? We have started to collect magnets for are project.*

6. What will you include in your presentation to convince your audience that your discoveries are valid? (Examples include pictures, videotapes, graphs, etc.)

*One of our parents will video tape us doing our reserch on magnets.*

Please sign below if you are willing to present your findings at the Kids Inquiry Conference© in May, 1995. You will be notified if the committee accepts your application.

Thank you.

*Beth Hickey, Maureen Riley, Lindsay Barron*
signature of applicant

Teachers noted the great care that children took completing the forms—striving to carefully and accurately document their responses, checking for perfect grammar, and using their best penmanship. Students were trying very hard to impress the KIC© committee, which, little did they know, the applications were read only by the classroom teacher.

For the students, the application process provided an air of professionalism, instilled a sense of responsibility, helped to clarify ideas, and provided the chance to reflect on and value past experiences. For the teachers, who were always searching out ways to "step back," responding to the applications allowed them to comment and raise questions in a less directive manner: "Have you decided how you will . . . ?"; "What books will you use to support your research?"; "What do you think would happen if you . . . ?"

The application process served other purposes as well. It was during this early period of KIC© preparation that Veronica made key decisions about how she would structure her students' involvement. Like Charlie and Susan, Veronica was concerned that her students might not be up to the challenge of formally presenting their research. But unlike the other two teachers, whose students were nurtured in safe and enriched environments and taught in adequately supplied classrooms, Veronica felt that she shouldered added responsibilities—to KIC©, to her students, and to the school community.

Her circumstances were not dissimilar to those of other urban schools—high student-teacher ratio, few school or home resources, and low parental involvement. Veronica knew that these factors often contribute to low self-esteem and decreased expectations for children, and she feared her students would have less confidence and poise in public situations than their KIC© colleagues. She did not want these young scientists, whom she knew were curious and intelligent people, to be overwhelmed.

Originally, Veronica planned to have a sampling of students from all her middle school science classes attend the conference and hoped that most of them would make presentations. But as she met with them during class time and after school, and as she thought about their unique situation in the KIC© community, she decided to concentrate her efforts on a small class of students she met with for an extended period each day. This way, she could focus her attention and resources on a manageable number of children and their investigations, help them secure additional resources, and even offer them extra time after school. Before long, it was obvious that these students had keen and varied interests and were anxious to meet the challenges of KIC©.

"I lived. I multiplied. I died. . . . But I loved oatmeal," wrote one of Veronica's students as a description of his research into the life cycles of mealworms. Spurred on by the story about insects and small creatures that Mrs. Stokes had read to the class, and an ample supply of mealworms and oatmeal, this student began reading, observing, and experimenting. He kept a supply of mealworms on his desk and at his home. He passed out baggies filled with mealworms and oatmeal to his friends. He reported weekly to the class about his discoveries.

As expected, KIC© preparation encouraged Veronica's sixth graders to become resourceful in tracking down materials, resources, and assistance. After an astronomy unit, several girls wanted to design a space station. The school's art teacher provided a room, materials and supplies, and extended the time in art class for the young space architects. Designing and building their own station raised lots of new questions for these students, not the least of which was what types of toilet facilities are used in space travel?

Veronica's students took tremendous initiative in looking beyond the classroom for answers to their queries. They contacted NASA and received printed material that described how space suits and vehicles are designed to accommodate all facets of personal hygiene. Innovative facilities were soon worked into the students' space station design and a new interest developed—space suit construction. Two girls again contacted NASA and were mailed samples of fabric used in space suits. Their project combined a needs analysis of space suit construction, research into past and current designs, and creative designs of their own.

In Susan's class, the application process was mandatory for all—every student was required to be part of an investigation team. Each child helped in the research and preparation of a KIC© presentation, but only those who wished to present before an audience would have to do so.

Earlier in the year, Susan's class had taken part in the National Geographic "JASON" project, an interactive teleconference which involved technology, undersea exploration, and solar energy. These themes were evident in all of the 1993 Carroll Manor KIC© projects. One group conducted an in-depth study on whales. Another demonstrated how radio signals are transmitted underwater and through the atmosphere.

Several students personalized their study of solar energy, setting out to make a solar oven that would cook hot dogs. They found directions in a book and built a parabola-shaped oven from cardboard and foil. It looked impressive, but the boys were disappointed when the oven temperature didn't get hot enough to actually cook anything. Now the question arose, could they make an oven that really *would* cook hot dogs?

Gathering the facts that they had learned about solar collectors and solar energy, the boys set out to build an oven of their own design. Their first step was to change the shape of the "collector" so that it was deeper and narrower. A stainless steel cooking bowl fit the bill exactly. They then placed this bowl into a deep box that they had painted flat black and covered it with a piece of glass "borrowed" from a picture frame.

Success! Their new oven was hot enough to cook hot dogs, a treat they shared with their classmates, teacher, and principal. Comparing the shapes and functionability of the two solar ovens they built became the scientific basis of their presentation.

## The Conference: Coming Together

As the KIC© date approached, KIC© committee meetings became more frequent, and with each meeting new questions arose. Each teacher was anxious to hear how the others were handling their KIC© preparation. And it was time to make decisions. How would the research projects be grouped? How long should each session last in order to provide enough time for presentation and follow-up discussions? Who could moderate the sessions? How would students choose the sessions they wanted to attend? How could scheduling this many students be accomplished?

It was decided that, as with professional conferences, each group of students would write a title and description for their session. Like an advertisement, these blurbs would be written to entice other student-scientists to attend. At the same time, the committee began grouping together two or three sessions that were related in some way. Sometimes this was easy. The mealworm research of Veronica's student was a neat fit with the two mealworm projects from Charlie's class.

"Space Station Winston" complemented another Manchester Elementary session, titled, "Fossils on Mars." The fossils presentation linked two areas of science that Charlie's students had encountered earlier in the year. During a unit on rocks and minerals, Charlie had brought in rock samples that were almost guaranteed to yield real fossils. Later in the year, during a solar system unit, several students had done significant reading and research into the planet Mars. Now they wondered—could there be fossils on Mars?

Tying together everything they knew about fossils (their chemistry as well as the conditions necessary for fossil formation and preservation) with what they'd discovered about Mars (surface and atmospheric conditions, similarities and differences to Earth, and the possibilities of life on the planet) they formulated an educated and convincing argument. Direct experience, solid research, and an intuitive leap all played important roles in this discussion.

Coupling concrete projects like Space Station Winston with more abstract ones like Fossils on Mars required some adult facilitation. Moderators were needed at each session to introduce speakers, monitor discussions, provoke questions, and help students make connections among the various research topics.

Things were falling into place. Excitement mounted. The day promised to be inviting, engaging, and rife with learning potential. Besides the break-out sessions, Charlie's students were planning the hands-on activities for KIC© participants. Campus tours were lined up so that students could see professional research scientists at work in physics, chemistry, or biology labs.

No one would be able to do it all! During the 10:30 session alone, students had to choose between:

## A. Protein in Your Cereal

*Death of a Mealworm* (Winston Middle)
I lived, I multiplied, I died. . . . But I loved oatmeal!
*Mealworms: Habitat and Diet* (Manchester Elementary)
What do you do if you can't find information on a bug you like? Research it yourself! See how a group of students gathered data about this interesting creature.
*Mealworms: Length of Life Stages* (Manchester Elementary)
How long does a mealworm live in your oatmeal? What stages of life does it go through?

## B. Looking for a Home

*Sealed Terrariums* (Manchester Elementary School)
How could people live on the moon? A sealed terrarium is a possible solution. By using mealworms a scientist determines if a sealed terrarium could work. Come see Sealed Terrariums . . . you could be looking at your future home.
*The Life People Didn't Know Existed* (Carroll Manor)
What can survive tremendous pressures and temperatures and can live in total darkness? People used to think that life didn't exist in space . . . or on the ocean floor. We now know differently about one of these!

## C. Pushing the Limits

*The Journey* (Carroll Manor)
What's longer than a bus, weighs more than four African elephants, eats using baleen and travels farther than from Maryland to Canada every year? Find out in this session.
*Aquatic Habitats* (Winston Middle)
Ouch, I'm too hot!
*The Effects of Salt Water on Plant Life* (Manchester Elementary)

Earth has a lot of water but almost all of it is salty. Can salt
water support plants on land? This team of scientists studied
how much salt some plants can tolerate.

D. *Hands-on Surprise* (Manchester Elementary)

E. *Campus Lab Tour*—Chemistry Lab

As May 27 approached, students in each class spent more and
more time making charts, posters, graphs, overheads, slides, or videos to
document their work. Veronica met with her students after school. Susan's
students rehearsed by giving their presentations to a class of fourth
graders. When not polishing their own presentations, Charlie's students
diligently prepared the sand mountain, earthquake machine, and eroding
river that they would bring for the hands-on session.

Several days before the conference, students in each class completed Kid-KIC©-Cards. Designed to be used as business cards, they
were imprinted with the school address and phone number. Students
added their names to the front of the cards and wrote a little about their
science questions and interests on the back. They were encouraged to ask
for the cards of students whose work they were especially interested in
and distribute their own cards to people they would like to have contact
them.

Although the true story of KIC© is primarily what happens before and after the conference—valuing and acting on children's curiosities; helping students develop testable questions; establishing time for
investigation and exploration; connecting reading, research, writing,
and documentation to the processes of science; building a climate for
student responsibility and self-confidence—the actual day of the conference is what may be best remembered by all involved. When the quiet
cafeteria exploded into a bustle of one hundred twenty students and
their teachers and chaperons, the long-dreamed-of possibilities became
reality.

Students shared, listened, and questioned. They joined in discussions with children they would not normally have had the opportunity to interact with. Several (but not many) even exchanged Kid-KIC©-Cards with
children from other schools. Tours of campus labs allowed student-scientists
to see the tools and processes used by professionals, and guest speakers provided the views of a university president and a professional writer.

Teachers and staff left satisfied . . . and bursting with many questions. Could they capture the magic a second time? Could KIC© '93 serve as a model for future conferences? Would it work for other groups of students, such as older or younger children or classes from different schools?

## Year 2: Revisiting the KIC© Process

Before the dust had settled on that first Kids' Inquiry Conference, plans began for KIC© '94. Everyone agreed to keep the same general format: break-out sessions in which the children could share their research with other students, a hands-on area, lab tours, keynote speakers, and a university campus setting.

There would be, however, several significant changes. First, the committee decided to move the conference date from May to March. Second, student-scientists would write up their research in a publication distributed to all KIC© classrooms. Finally, another class of children would be added to increase the pool of research and add to the number of children who would benefit from KIC© involvement.

The original expectation for KIC© was that student research was to be presented as works-in-progress, not as finished products. Elementary school science is too often presented in neat, complete packages. Frequently, classroom instruction is conducted in units that include, perhaps, some hands-on activities that lead students to meet some previously agreed-upon learning outcome. A culminating project might be added to demonstrate mastery of a concept, repeating previously discovered facts. Loose ends are tied up. All questions are answered. The unit is packed away.

Real science investigation is much messier. Research is ongoing. The answer to one question only leads investigators to new questions. Hypotheses are not always proven, but seemingly "wrong" answers point out new directions to explore.

Whether they are studying cosmology, environmental issues, or AIDS, professional scientists attend conferences to share where they are in a lifetime of research and to get new insights into their investigations. They present their findings-to-date and listen to others searching out clues to the same or similar questions.

The 1993 KIC© conference, held at the end of May, left little school time for a child to extend research, to act on comments and questions offered by scientists in the audience, or to explore something completely new that he or she had encountered at the conference. Holding the conference in March would encourage and allow more students to present their findings while still in the middle of their research, so rooms were reserved for March 16, 1994.

Everyone felt that the students needed to document their research more thoroughly than they had for the first conference. Many students had used slides, videos, graphs, and charts to accompany their KIC© '93 projects, but few had written up their findings. Consequently, there was no chronicle of student investigations that could be referenced by future KIC© scientists.

The write-ups would also add to the more immediate learning experience. Writing about their questions, procedures, and findings would help students make sense of what they were doing. At some points, the process would flag areas that required clarification and further research. At others, it would help children establish replicable steps that they, or other student-scientists, could follow to test and retest results. Writing might even lead to new ideas, provoke new questions, or generate new investigations.

The committee decided that entries for a *Kids' Inquiry Conference© Science Journal* would be required of all students presenting at the conference. This, they decided, added another authentic piece to the KIC© picture, further validating the students' efforts as scientists.

The final change was easily accomplished. Maureen Hoyer, who teaches in suburban Baltimore County, signed up her Woodbridge Elementary fourth-grade students. But, as in science, where the solution to one problem leads to new questions, the addition of Maureen's fourth graders raised new questions among the KIC© committee. Would KIC© work with students this young? Could they participate on equal footing with fifth- and sixth-grade students? Would the research of a ten-year-old convince an eleven-, twelve-, or even thirteen-year-old? Would it be interesting? Would they be able to effectively document what they had done?

It was soon obvious that Maureen's students would be capable and convincing scientists. Maureen decided to require every one of her students to not only participate in an investigation, but to stand up and present at the upcoming conference. They dug right in. Their weekly inquiry periods were animated sessions in which individuals, pairs, and small groups hauled out the microscopes, batteries, bicycle pumps, and cameras. They investigated molds, oils, balloons, and water. Several tested consumer products found in their homes.

One fourth-grade contribution to the *1994 Kids' Inquiry Conference© Journal* provides a sampling of their research topics. The journal entry also offers insight into how KIC© participants come up with their ideas; how their notions of fair testing evolved; how by "failing" to produce a desired outcome, they actually learned; and how they realized that their investigations were works-in-progress.

### The Battery Group

*Zac Hunt, Ryan Baker, Daniel Morsberger & Mike Rowe*

**Introduction.** The Battery Group got started when Ryan was changing the batteries in his Game Gear™. He thought why buy a battery when you can make one? When Ryan told his friends Zac and Mike, they wondered what is in a battery to make it work? Then Daniel came in the group, we worked on experiments with batteries.

**Procedure.** First for our research, we read books about batteries and how to make a battery. The books we read were *Batteries, Bulbs and Wires* and *Electricity*. Next we tried to answer the questions, "which batteries last the longest, Duracell™ or Energizer™?" and "how can you make a battery?"

We worked on answering the first question. We tried to answer the question which battery lasts longest? The batteries we were testing were Energizer™ and Duracell™. Mike tested Energizer™ in a bunny and he tested Duracell™ in a Walkman™. So while we're not sure what battery really lasted the longest, from that test Energizer™ lasted the longest. Mike should have tested the batteries in the bunny or the Walkman™.

Then we tried to make our own battery. We read about a battery you could make using a dime, a penny, wire, blotting paper, thumbtacks, tape, a board, compass, and salt water. But first we needed to make a conductor. We wrapped wire around the cup that we used for the salt water. Then we taped and tacked down the coiled wire onto the board. Next, we stripped off one half inch of the insulation on each end of the wire. We did that because then we could touch the wire directly to the penny and the dime.

Next we wet a piece of blotting paper in saltwater. Then we stuck a penny on one side of the blotting paper and a dime on the other side. We set a compass on top of the wrapped wire. Finally we connected the wire to the penny and the dime, and the reaction should have been that the compass needle would spin. Look at Appendix 1 [Figure 13–1] for a picture of the materials.

**Results.** This battery wasn't a complete success. We tried changing our variables one at a time, but our battery didn't work. We think that the problem was that the copyright date of the book where we read about the battery was 1968. We found out that dimes were made of different metals back then, and we figured this was why our battery wouldn't work.

Interestingly, it was two of Maureen's fourth graders who came up with the first behavioral science research project at KIC©. Megan and Kristen decided to observe the habits of toddlers watching television, specifically asking which children's television program best holds children's attention. As they conducted their research, they struggled with such sophisticated notions as: What observable behavior constituted evidence that their subjects were interested in a particular program? What conclusions could they draw from that evidence? Even though their questions were established early, Megan and Kristen, like many scientists before them, soon learned that research does not always run smoothly.

As in other KIC© classrooms, Maureen's students usually met in self-selected groups. Rather than working with best friends or children whose personalities, abilities, and skills closely matched their own, these students were more likely to partner with those sharing similar interests and questions. Once groups were formed, specific roles (recorder, observer, materials collector, encourager) were never assigned by a teacher. Instead, group members would have to make many decisions on their own: How would they gather materials, conduct research, control variables, collect data? How would they reach consensus? Who would give the final presentation?

Kristen and Megan quickly discovered that their work habits, like their personalities and talents, were very different. After great debate, they decided to conduct (as they stated in the introduction to their KIC© journal report) "parallel research and combined [their] results at the end."

Kristen gathered information by developing and distributing a

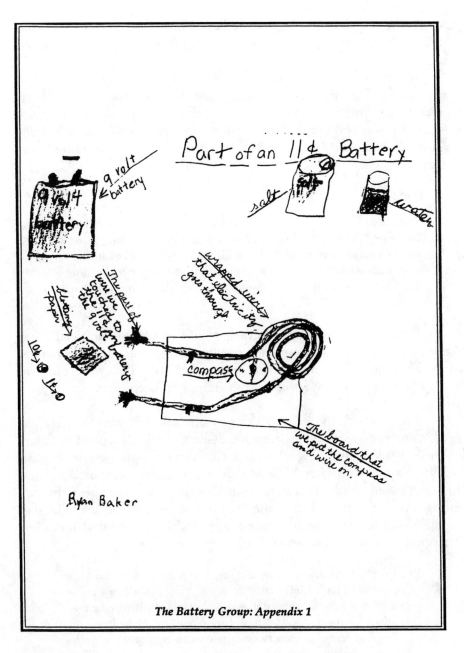

*The Battery Group: Appendix 1*

**FIGURE 13–1**

questionnaire to several mothers of toddlers. Then she recorded how many minutes each child watched each program and drew her conclusions from that.

Megan decided to directly observe children, visiting each one several times. She identified behavior she believed indicated interest (dances along, sings along, smiles, sits, takes a nap, walks away, lies down, and cries) and graphed the results. She also kept a log of her observations, and quickly learned that such strategies often presented new problems:

> **2/24**
>
> We asked Carolyn if she liked Sesame Street or Barney better. She said "Barney." Then we asked if she liked Sesame Street or Lambchop better, and she said, "Barney." This is important because on the chart it shows that she spent more time watching Lambchop and Sesame Street than she watched Barney.

Finally, the girls combined their results to write their conclusion: "As you can see from our combined results, Barney was the favorite television program." Their research recommendations? "If any of you have any brothers or sisters, we recommend Barney to keep them out of your hair."

KIC© '94 finally arrived. Once again, students were actively engaged in student-to-student sharing, hands-on activities (supplied by Charlie's fifth graders and several of Karen Pearce's eighth-grade English students from Westminster West Middle School), and campus lab tours. This time noted children's author Jean Craighead George spent the day visiting with students and was the featured afternoon speaker. The day was filled with magic moments, the essence of which is captured in this letter written by a parent-chaperon.

> I've been on my share of field trips, but none where the kids *were* the field trip! I have been to science fairs (always a competition) but not one where it was a sharing of information—no right or wrong, good or bad, first place [or] last place.
>
> A great learning experience, just working together, gathering information, charting, drawing pictures, all things that these children are going to need in [the future].

## The Next Step: Meeting a Wider Audience

Now, with several wonderful KIC© experiences behind them; a cadre of excited children, satisfied parents, and supportive administrators spreading the word; and documentation on film and in print of kids doing authentic science research; the KIC© committee stands convinced that this is a valuable and replicable activity. But in ESIP, "to replicate" does not mean simply to repeat or to clone an activity. Where would, could, and should the concept of KIC© go from here? How can it evolve? How can it be adapted to suit the needs of a greater audience? What should be the next step?

The new KIC© questions have become: What can we learn about setting up a larger-scale KIC© program? Would it be possible to have a local or regional "KIC© Week," in which children from both ESIP and non-ESIP classrooms take part in some KIC©-type sharing and reporting of their own research, based on their own questions and investigations?

The KIC© committee realizes that they have had advantages through grant-funding and their connections with a research university. It would have been very difficult indeed to get KIC© up and running so quickly without these resources. But does this mean it cannot happen elsewhere?

In an effort to make KIC© more easily replicated by others, several changes were successfully instituted in 1995. Funding was secured from Becton Dickinson, a local scientific research and development corporation. These funds paid for buses and room fees, and subsidized part of the *1995 Kids' Inquiry Conference Science Research Journal* publication costs (students raised money to cover the remaining KIC© journal fees).

To accommodate the increased number of teachers who wished to participate, the campus-based KIC© '95 took place over two days. Science lab tours were omitted on one of those days and replaced with additional break-out and poster sessions, thus building on the notion that KIC©'s true mission is to provide a forum for students to share with other students. The keynote speakers were less famous than those of the previous years, but proved to be affordable and interesting. Thursday's speaker came from the education department of a local museum and Friday's from a nearby NASA facility (NASA speakers are available at no cost in many areas across the country).

Finally, authentic evidence that KIC© is viable as an off-campus program occurred in late May when pen pals from two Baltimore County elementary schools met at a local park facility and held the *Kids' Inquiry*

*Conference at Sherwood Farm.* As expected, the science, sharing, and excitement closely paralleled that of the university-based conferences. The Sherwood Farms planners used the 1993 and 1994 conference as models, adapting the campus-based structure to suit their specific student interests and conference needs. Consequently, many fresh and innovative ideas were added to the KIC© process.

## The Legacy of KIC©

No one knows exactly what will be remembered by the students involved in KIC©. Most will probably remember an event—the campus, the sessions, a science labs tour, the hands-on activities, or a keynote speaker. Many will clearly remember the details of their own research or the interesting elements of a session they attended. But surely, we hope, the true legacy of KIC© involvement will prove to be an awareness of the scientific processes and the energy that builds as scientists, young or old, question, investigate, discover . . . and question again.

The significance of KIC© is the opportunity to foster those elements so vital to classroom practice: time, trust, choice, and authenticity. It is the time for students to pursue extended, often year-long, investigations that frequently change direction and take new forms. It is a child's risky navigation through charted and uncharted territory anchored by a teacher's support and trust and guidance. It is students learning to rely on themselves and one another. And finally, it is a forum that allows young people to value their own curiosities and see themselves as capable researchers, articulate speakers, able thinkers, and valuable human beings.

## Bibliography

Charles Pearce interview by Barbara Bourne, audiotape, Nov. 19, 1994.

McDonald, B. 1957. *Hello, Mrs. Piggle Wiggle.* Philadelphia: Lippincott.

Pearce, C. 1993. "What If . . . ?" In *Science Workshop: A Whole Language Approach*, ed. W. Saul et al. Portsmouth, NH: Heinemann.

# About the Contributors

**Barbara Bourne** is Program Director of the Elementary Science Integration Project (ESIP). She is coauthor of *Exploring Space: Using Seymour Simon's Astronomy Books in the Classroom* (Morrow Junior Books, 1994) and of *Thinking Like Mathematicians: Putting the K–4 NCTM Standards into Practice* (Heinemann 1994).

**Debra Bunn** is a sixth-grade teacher at Corkran Middle School in Anne Arundel County, Maryland. She can be seen in the Elementary Science Integration Project's video, *Thinking Science* (Heinemann 1995). Debra began her squid unit as a fifth-grade teacher at Meade Heights Elementary School. She is a former ESIP Staff Teacher.

**Barbara Caplan** has taught elementary school in Baltimore County, Maryland for twenty-three years. She currently teaches fifth grade at Franklin Elementary School. She is a former ESIP Staff Teacher.

**Linda Davis** has taught elementary school for seventeen years. She currently teaches fourth grade at the Friends School in Baltimore, Maryland. Linda is an avid hiker, botanist, and bird-watcher.

**Donna Dieckman** teaches first grade at Greenwood Elementary School in Montgomery County, Maryland. She is a coauthor of the Reference Guide for *Find It! Science*, a database of children's science trade books on CD-

ROM (Follett Software Company 1996), and serves as a reviewer for the NSTA/Children's Book Council *Outstanding Science Trade Books for Children* award.

**Carol Flicker** is a first-grade teacher at Hutchison Elementary School in Fairfax County, Virginia, where she has also taught second grade. She recently spent a summer as an intern at Nancie Atwell's Center for Teaching and Learning in Edgecombe, Maine.

**Twig C. George,** a writer, educator, and ESIP Project Associate, has just published her first children's book, *A Dolphin Named Bob* (HarperCollins 1996). Her interest in science and writing stems from childhood. She was raised in a family of artists, writers, and scientists and has always found the combination inspiring.

**Mary Beth Johnson** is currently a science resource teacher at Greencastle Elementary School in Montgomery County, Maryland. She is also a coauthor of the Reference Guide for *Find It! Science* (Follett Software Company 1996). "Looking for Hope in All the Wrong Places" describes her experiences as a fourth-grade classroom teacher in Montgomery County Schools.

**Carole Roberts** has taught grades K–2 for Montgomery County Public Schools in Maryland. She was teaching kindergarten at Greenwood Elementary when she wrote the journal entries that resulted in "The Building Blocks of Science."

**Stephanie Terry** is a longtime Baltimore City educator, currently teaching first grade at Ashburton Elementary School in Baltimore, Maryland. She can be seen in the Elementary Science Integration Project's video, *Thinking Science* (Heinemann 1995), and has been featured in several episodes of *Teacher to Teacher with Mr. Wizard,* which airs on Nickelodeon.